A.Z

"Delightful sport! whose never failing charm,
Makes young blood tingle and keeps old blood warm."
G. Colman.

Experiences
OF
Flagellation

A Series of Remarkable Instances of Whipping
Inflicted on Both Sexes,

WITH

CURIOUS ANECDOTES OF LADIES

FOND OF ADMINISTERING BIRCH DISCIPLINE.

COMPILED BY

AN AMATEUR FLAGELLANT.

Fredonia Books
Amsterdam, The Netherlands

Experiences of Flagellations:
A Series of Remarkable Instances of Whipping
Inflicted on Both Sexes

Compiled by
An Amateur Flagellant

ISBN: 1-4101-0383-8

Reprinted from the 1885 edition

Fredonia Books
Amsterdam, The Netherlands
http://www.fredoniabooks.com

In order to make original editions of historical works available to scholars at an economical price, this facsimile of the original edition of 1885 is reproduced from the best available copy and has been digitally enhanced to improve legibility, but the text remains unaltered to retain historical authenticity.

EXPERIENCES

OF

FLAGELLATION.

CORPORAL PUNISHMENT, &c.

We have received from time to time numerous letters respecting punishment at schools, and these letters, as is generally the case upon every subject of controversy, contain every variety of opinion thereon.

The subject is modern; our ancestors never disputed the propriety and utility of corporal punishment. But the age of refinement, indulgence, and mercy seems to be dawning, and minds that are disposed to ultra views and illogical excesses, have no sooner seen the feeble glimmerings of its light, than they begin to urge the immediate adoption of such modes and systems of social behaviour and discipline as can only be realised in a millennial sunshine.

We are glad to see the spirit of mercy dawning upon the world. It is ominous of good. We have no doubt whatsoever that it will continue to increase "like the morning light that shineth more and more unto the perfect day," and that the time will come, when the real character of humanity being better understood, and the temptations of the poor, and the incapacity of the feeble-minded, being more charitably described by public writers and pulpit preachers, society at large will address itself more earnestly than heretofore to the task of removing those temptations, and cultivating the talents which are prone to action, however humble in their rank of being, instead of forcing into a state of activity and authority faculties so constitutionally weak, as evidently to be intended by Nature to be passive for life.

But in the meantime, we must not run too fast, nor begin to speak our Italian whilst we are travelling through France; we must wait till we have passed the Alps.

Moreover, there is great danger always in jumping hastily to a conclusion. Having found ourselves wrong in one extreme, we show great logical weakness in leaping over to the other. Reformed drunkards become austere apostles of abstinence—they abhor the sight of a bottle; even a cork inspires them with a sermon against fermentation, forgetting that they themselves during the heat of the discourse are most notable examples of it. A parson who turns infidel rails with more than usual acerbity against his former faith. And the infidel who is converted becomes an inordinate zealot; such another *good* parson, in some people's eyes, as a reformed rake is a *good* husband in the estimation of some ladies who know no better. For our own part, we dislike all extremes, and are determined always to seek for justice, not in one or the other scale, but at the fulcrum of the balance.

That God has ordained corporal punishment no man can doubt. Even the atheist allows that Nature has ordained it. Moreover, it is ordained for discipline and government; every animal is governed by it; every animal understands it and fears it; and the fear of it keeps every creature in its own sphere, and for ever prevents that natural confusion and disorder that would instantly arise without it. The burnt child dreads the fire and keeps out of it. This law of Nature is indispensable. If the child felt no pain, and the fire still retain its natural consuming qualities, the child would be destroyed or its clothes would be consumed. And if the fire were divested of its consuming properties it would cease to be fire. We cannot imagine an improvement upon this system. The Divine law of government by pain is admirable, and we all know from experience, that it is perfectly compatible with a state of pure social felicity. Though fire burns, and inflicts severe punishment upon every one who wantonly touches it, yet we all keep it, and cherish it, and approach it even with fondness; we use it, and learn by the severity and even the cruelty of its discipline not to abuse it. We have no desire to make fire less cruel than it is; this would destroy its utility. Our duty is to respect its authority, and teach our children to respect it; for so long as we treat it with respect, it will deal very gently and tenderly with us. It is the most sacred material type of God himself, who is severe as fire, if you transgress His immutable and inviolable laws; but gentle as warmth if you do not.

We are all subject to this Divine government of pain, without a single exception. It belongs to the physical department —the police department of our mundane system; a moral government without it could have no existence, and an intellectual government without it is an absurdity. Physical, moral, and intellectual, are three in one and one in three, mutually dependent on one another We cannot escape the physical discipline as parents. Why should we attempt to emancipate our children from it?

But it may be replied, "Why not leave the children to that Divine law of physical discipline to which we ourselves are subject?" We reply by another question, "Why not leave them altogether, and teach them nothing at all?" They are given in charge to us in order that we may teach them the nature of the Divine law, and prepare them for manhood and womanhood. And it is just this very Divine law in all its varieties, so far as they are applicable to moral government, that constitutes the most important lesson that they have to learn from us. To teach them some fanciful, whimsical sentimentalism of our own conception, will only prevent their reasoning faculties. It will teach them to reason falsely respecting Nature and its everlasting ordinances, and take away from them the very rudder with which they steer their course on the ocean of life. The Divine law and the holy fear of that law, is the beginning of wisdom. Corporal chastisement for folly is an everlasting feature of that law. What then will a child learn from a parent whose system is at variance with the Divine law, and who attempts to effect his purpose only by intellectual and moral means, without the use of the physical? It will soon learn, the most unpalatable truth for both parties, that its parent is an incongruity, pursuing a whim which is not in accordance with the laws of God as established in the world in which we live.

Our fair correspondent, "Charlotte," says, "If personal punishment be abolished, what punishment is to replace it? Low diet and confinement? The children have already quite enough of the former, and our girls too much of the latter." But if either of these two be employed, it is physical and corporal punishment. Low diet punishes the body—it punishes the palate. Confinement punishes both body and mind. It tends very much to weaken the mental and moral faculties. We should rather give a boy a good smart birching, and let him off, to play at cricket or marbles, than immure him an hour in a solitary dungeon or school-room. The former will keep alive the spirit of the boy; the other, if frequently repeated, would enfeeble his intellect and make him a dunce.

"I was three years," says Charlotte, "at a school where no personal punishment was to be inflicted. There I acquired much pertness, and a large quantity of self-conceit. Notwithstanding her protestations to the contrary, the school-mistress was several times compelled to inflict severe punishment, but always did it in private. The little I ever learnt, was in a school where the lesson must be completed, or the punishment endured. I was idle, conceited, with an imagination excited by the constant reading of novels, &c. Two or three applications of the birch humbled my pride, dispelled my romantic notions, and stimulated me to exertions that else I had never made. It was not the pain; that I could endure. It was the idea of such an important personage as myself figuring in so unheroic a character as that of a whipped dunce, which determined me to make every exertion to avoid so unpleasant an exhibition."

Children are naturally the subjects of the physical government, more than of the intellectual and the moral The first is understood almost at birth, and is comprehended by every species of animal. It is the most universal of all systems of discipline; the basis of all government. It is, however, for that very reason the lowest species of government. Many animals, perhaps, are incapable of rising above it; and few, except those that are trained by man, can be made to exhibit any symptoms of understanding the moral and intellectual training. A chicken fears as soon as it makes its escape from the egg; a child fears at its mother's breast, long before the moral or intellectual nature has revealed even the dawn of its existence. Selfishness, a purely animal passion, arises before generosity. "Me! me! me!" is the soul of a child, and its selfishness is only beautiful and interesting because it is feeble and governable. But give a child the strength of a man, with nothing more than its own childish nature, and it would prove a frightful monster.* It would smash everything to atoms, and murder every one in the house. Its feebleness and helplessness are our protection in its purely physical state of existence, before the intellectual and the moral natures have begun to define themselves.

In such a state of being, physical training is all-important, but not corporal punishment; for the infant does not understand it. By physical training, we mean the proper treatment of the child's body, in respect to personal comfort, or food, clothing, and temperature. To make the child comfortable, is the first object of consideration; but if the child require medicine, it must be administered, though unpalatable; and if the child require a surgical operation, it must be performed. It must not be fed on sugar, even if it relish it; and it must not be allowed to put its hands into treacle and suck its fingers. Even if it cry for permission thus to enjoy itself it must be forbidden. It is forbidden gently at first, because of its want of understanding; but when the child is old enough to understand a frown and a stern refusal, it must receive them. If it did not, it would not be properly instructed; because frowns and rebukes are amongst "the powers that be, and which are ordained by God;" powers that the child must come in contact with in after life, and, therefore, powers with which it must be made acquainted, so soon as it is able to understand their legitimate meaning. But in teaching the child the meaning of these frowns and rebukes, they should always be associated with the idea of a wrong committed; for then they have a moral meaning, and having a moral meaning, they have a moral effect. But frowns without a moral meaning must be morally injurious, because they are unjust.

Frowns precede punishment, like dawn before the morning. Should they prove sufficient for a child, it is well; the discipline then is effectual. But they will not always prove so, not even with very timid children; and perhaps it is not a very favourable symptom of a child's spirit, when it can always be cowed with a look. It symptomises an amiable, but not an energetic disposition. When the frown is not sufficient to prevent disobedience, what comes next? Reason? Have you got

---

The Brobdignagian child put Gulliver in its mouth, in order to eat him. Fortunately for the traveller, its intention was defeated! A beautiful parable, or truth in the form of a fable.

it? or has the child got it? Do your best with it. But be quick, for obedience must be immediate. The house must not be kept in an uproar, waiting for the logical conclusion of a debate between you and a refractory boy. Moreover, even when such a rational termination of the controversy is obtained, you have not maintained your parental authority; on the contrary, an equality is established between you and the child. You have merely come to terms. And such is the nature of all undisciplined minds, that a refractory child, even when reasoned into compliance, generally considers that it has done you a favour—that it has merely been doing an act of condescension, and that the victory belongs to it and not to you. The next controversy very probably demonstrates this; and in the course of a few years it jumps to conclusions without listening to argument; and then you resort to entreaty, and supplication, and even to tears, as indulgent mothers very often do, and thus humble and degrade yourselves before your own subjects. This is not the way to preserve parental authority, or respect for parental authority; but it is a consummation you are very likely to attain to with refractory and obstinate children, of strong passions, domineering tempers, and selfish dispositions, if you neglect in their education that fundamental law of physical discipline which God has ordained for ever in His own government, and which you, as a whimsical philosopher, attempting to improve upon His laws, have tried to dispense with.

Now, a parent or teacher who pledges himself never to use the rod, does violence to the Divine law, and deprives the child of the benefit of that holy fear which is an indispensable feature of all moral government. But it is equally true, that a parent or a teacher who resorts immediately to physical punishment with a child that has attained the age at which moral and intellectual discipline may be understood, is merely a tyrant. The fear, as Charlotte remarks, is the proper stimulant; and that fear can only exist when the law that begets it has a being. Repeal the law, and the fear dies along with it. We were seven years, altogether, at two schools, where corporal punishment was daily inflicted; and we have so often recalled to remembrance and recounted the castigations we received, that we believe we can enumerate them all—they amounted only to four. Four castigations in seven years! We were always afraid of them, being very sensitive to pain; and we were always ashamed of them at the same time, being equally sensitive to shame. On one occasion we were pilloried; being put up on a sort of scaffold, with a huge barrister's or counsellor's wig on our head, and, as a loud burst of laughter arose from the assembled scholars, we burst into tears. Some boys would caper and make fun in such circumstances; the wig, of course, would be no punishment to them. Where the wig would suffice, it would be better than the rod; because it is a higher order of punishment, being less physical and more intellectual and moral. But where it would not suffice, it would be no punishment at all. And to treat two boys of different temperaments with the same species of discipline, is as absurd and immoral as that magisterial system of iniquity established in our police-courts, which fines a gentleman of ten thousand a-year five shillings for getting drunk, and a cobbler, with ten or fifteen shillings a week, the same. The rod should be held *in terrorem* over those whose perversity demands the application of it to their persons, but it should not be wantonly or frequently inflicted. It ought to be kept for the sake of the fear that it inspires; and that the child may not be suffered to flatter itself with personal impunity in case of misbehaviour. But its application should be a serious and a ceremonial action, which the school in silence should be called upon to witness—occasionally at least; and it should always be understood, that the physical discipline is only administered because the intellectual and the moral discipline have failed to be effectual in the particular case.

There are many in these sentimental and whimsical times who take the pledge not to use corporal punishment in the treatment of children, and who send them to school upon the express condition that they are not to be beaten, whatsoever be the offence.

There are others who are blessed with very mild and tractable children, who require no rude discipline, who are overawed by a look and commanded by a tone; and those are in the habit of informing their friends how very easily and skilfully they manage their children, without making use of bodily pain as a principle of parental government.

But the portraits of one man's children will not pass for every other man's; and to pledge ourselves not to whip a disobedient child who really deserves it, is really to pledge ourselves not to do our duty. "He that spareth the rod" on such an occasion, as Solomon, an old-fashioned philosopher, has remarked, "hateth the child."

In reasoning upon this, as upon all other subjects, with the generality of people, we are always sure to be entertained with a number of most outrageous examples, as of schoolmasters using rulers and knocking out boys' eyes, or using their clenched fists and striking them on the ears, stunning and making idiots of them, and such other monstrosities, which have nothing to do with the argument. For all parties condemn such conduct as tyrannical, and justly amenable to the criminal law. A schoolmaster who uses his clenched fist to strike a pupil, ought to be considered guilty of a criminal assault, unless the pupil has actually provoked the outrage by previously striking his master. But one who confines himself to the customary and legitimate modes of punishment sanctioned by tradition must not be identified with a felon, who listens only to his own irregular passions, and has no other system of punishment but that of revenge for the annoyance he has received.

We should not, therefore, reason with people who talk about rulers, and clenched fists, and other extremes, and make use of them as arguments to show the propriety of going to the opposite extreme. This is not logical reasoning. It is merely vulgar common-place conversational controversy, that terminates without a conclusion.

There are some who would make an exception in favour of girls, and leave the boys to the old rod, the birch, the cane, or the thong. This is unjust; we see no reason why they should be treated differently. Children are of no sex. Fourier calls them neuters. When the sex is formed, the distinction begins to be admitted. But why a boy of seven should be whipped and a girl of seven not whipped for an act of disobedience, is more than any logic that we are acquainted with can make apparent.

Ladies are treated delicately, not because they are of the feminine gender, but because their manners are delicate. But when a woman becomes an exception to her sex, we consider ourselves relieved from the general obligations of gallantry. If a gentleman met a very beautiful and elegantly dressed lady in the park, who accosted him and asked him the way to Buckingham House, he would treat her with all respect, and give her the required information if he could. But were such a lady to take him by the collar, and clench her fists and threaten him like a bully, his gallantry would naturally take a very different direction. In the one case the woman has behaved like a lady, and has received the treatment which lady-like behaviour deserves. In the other she has not behaved like a lady, and the gentleman would be justified in using her somewhat roughly.

It is in vain to plead in the latter case that the woman is a lady, and that it is considered ungallant and dishonourable in any gentleman to lay violent hands upon a woman. The woman has placed herself beyond the protection of the law of chivalry by unladylike behaviour. Her own sex would condemn her, and justify the gentleman, even if he bound her with a rope and took her home in a wheelbarrow. This is an extreme case, to show that extreme behaviour must always expect to meet with extreme treatment. Now young ladies are all (poetically and figuratively) supposed to be mild, gentle, tractable, beautiful, and amiable, and they generally appear to be so to the eye of the stranger. The parent and the governess often find them otherwise. So long as a parent and governess can reason the young lady into obedience, it is well to use no other argument. But when reason will not suffice, what must be done? We asked a young governess not long ago, what sorts of punishment she had seen in her experience, and she had been in several schools both in France and England. She said, she never saw corporal pnnishment inflicted. They were generally punished with a longer lesson, sometimes with a passage of Scripture to get by rote; sometimes they were sent to bed early, and sometimes confined. It seems they must be punished in some way or other. Now, all those modes of punishment are bad, for they are injurious to health. Much poring over books is very bad for young people. It is not very good for old folks. It is sedentary employment. It is dull and unsocial, and, when employed as a punishment, it leaves the young to the society of passions that are low, vicious, spiteful, and revengeful. A child shut up and condemned in solitude to a task, is a little live bottle filled with slow, deliberate, hatching malice. Moreover, to make education itself a punishment, is morally and mentally degrading to that very education we are so anxious to promote; and to punish a child by making it learn a chapter of the word of God, is to make the temple of God merely a house of correction, and to convert the Book of Books into a species of treadmill—a most pernicious practice, whose effects are visible enough in the general antipathy with which the Bible is regarded even in religious families. We would rather have a child well birched than well chaptered.

Some employ fines, which are no punishment to the rich, but sufficiently formidable to the poor. The poor alone, therefore, are benefited by fines, for they alone fear them. The rich man does not fear the fine at the police-court; he only fears the exposure in the public papers. To the poor man the fine is a serious matter, for if it be not paid the house of correction is perhaps the alternative. This system, so unequal in civil government, is equally unjust in schools, where there are always rich pupils who care nothing for it, and poor who regard it with trepidation. The former are apt to make fun of the latter, and either destroy their spirit, or drive them recklessly into wild and ruinous behaviour. This system has been very generally adopted in Scotch colleges, where there are always many poor students, to whom even a sixpenny fine is a severe punishment. It generally has the effect of producing punctual attendance and orderly behaviour, two indispensable prerequisites for successful teaching.

All possible modes of rewards and punishments, we believe, have been attempted, and all have been found more or less inefficient. It is not reasonable to suppose that one system can be adopted for all tempers. As a school is a collection of every variety of disposition, it is reasonable to suppose that every variety of discipline should prevail in it. A child who is meek and gentle at home, and easily managed by the look or word of a parent, is likely to be so at school also; and a parent ought not to be afraid of sending such a child to a school where corporal punishment is inflicted, for the child is not very likely ever to receive it. Whereas, a child who is unmanageable without corporal punishment, is not a very suitable subject for a mild government that never inflicts it. Such a child would corrupt a whole school, and must either be whipped or expelled. In reply to this, it is frequently urged that every child is accessible to reason, and may be managed without the rod, if the teacher only understood the proper method of coaxing. This we do not regard as true doctrine. It bears inaccuracy on its very front. It would argue an imperfection in universal humanity—a want of wisdom in the Creator Himself, were it so. It would be doing despite to His own physical government, thus to make all men capable of being governed by moral and intellectual motives. No, there are dispositions so purely or supremely physical by nature, that nothing but physical treatment will overcome the most vicious features of their dispositions. Moreover, we do not admire the system of exclusive coaxing. Nothing tends so much to create a peevish, pettish, and unsociable disposition, as coaxing in youth. Were the world a real coaxing world, then it would be judicious in parents to coax their children always. They would thus train them for the world into which they are born. But the world is not a coaxing world, and therefore the coaxing system is not a preparation for the world we live in. The world is a battle-field, an arena of fierce, of animated, or interested conflict. It is a world of authority and obedience, a world in which all must learn to obey before they can be authorised to govern; even the prince, who is born to rule, must first be subject; for many, if not all of the most amiable qualities of humanity are acquired or cultivated in the state of subjection. Now to coax a child is not to command, but to entreat it, to supplicate it, to set it on a throne and bow before it; a dangerous beginning, the source perhaps of a large amount of that offensive peevishness which beclouds the sunshine of the fairest assemblies, merely because a humour which has always been petted at home has found itself thwarted abroad. To learn obedience is, in our opinion, one of the most important branches of education, and this obedience on the one side, implies a command on the other. Our government preserves the form of this great natural truth in the court etiquette. The queen always commands, she does not entreat; "by her majesty's special command," the play of Othello is performed at the Haymarket or Drury lane; it is not at her majesty's request; and this, after all, is the pure paternal or patriarchal etiquette, an etiquette which is compatible with the greatest amount of respect and affection on the one hand, and of paternal dignity and authority on the other.

Now such authority is incompatible with coaxing, for coaxing implies that a child may or may not do what the parent wishes it to do. There are matters of minor importance, in respect to which authority relaxes itself and suffers coaxing with propriety, and even dignity, to exert its own peculiar talents: and such variety, which includes all the possible modes of government by love and fear, and all their combinations, is the very perfection of government. But an exclusive, one-sided, whimsical, sentimental system, which adopts one mode and rejects another, without taking into consideration the peculiar disposition of the child, is merely one of those extravagances which have been developed in this age of private opinion, have destroyed the old principle of authority in parents and teachers, and made boys and girls the smart, the heartless, and very often the just and reasonable critics of men and women.

If authority on one side and obedience on the other be indispensable, physical or corporal punishment must be employed; we do not say that it must be employed in every case, but the parent or teacher cannot take the pledge never to employ it. Coaxing, as we have already seen, is incompatible with authority. The idea of punishment is inseparable from authority; and if the offended or disobeyed parent do not employ the rod, he must inflict a privation that is equivalent to it. The child must be sent to bed an hour or two before its time! a very silly punishment, to say the least of it; or it must have no pudding! a very sensual punishment; or it must not go to the play!—this looks more intellectual, but it is very dangerous for the development of malicious passions; or it must learn a long lesson! and at the same time learn to curse the book which it ought to bless; or it must learn a chapter of the Bible, a hymn, or a psalm! thus quietly teaching it the elements of blasphemy and irreligion; or it must be birched! and thus taught the evil of bodily pain, and to choose the alternative of pain or obedience.

Now, it is evident that, if obedience be a good, it must be contrasted with an evil, as its penal alternative. If you contrast it with the apostles' creed, or a chapter of the Bible, then you make these penal alternatives, and therefore very bad things. If you contrast it with going to bed early, then you make "going early to bed" a bad thing. If you contrast it with "not going to the play," then you make "not going to the play" a bad thing. If you contrast it with "no pudding," then you make "no pudding," a bad thing. If you contrasted it with "bodily pain," then you make "bodily pain" a bad thing. Now, which of all these things is most truly and most indisputably bad? There is only one of them respecting which all parties agree, and that is the bodily pain. It is a bad thing; it is an evil; and, for that very reason, it is a legitimate species of punishment.

But, again : to punish well you must punish in such a manner as to effect your purpose, and not to injure the child, either bodily, mentally, or morally. When corporal punishment injures the child, it is illegitimate. It is then revenge, not educational discipline. When it injures the moral or intellectual nature, it is equally wrong. Moreover, when it destroys love between you and the child, it is injudicious. Punishment, to be sacred and efficient, must cultivate the spirit and the courage, stimulate the ardour and activity of the child, correct its vicious habits, purify its language, polish its manners, cultivate its mind, and increase its respect and affection for its teacher. It is a difficult thing to punish well. Few teachers thoroughly understand it. And when they do not, even severity itself cannot enforce discipline. Love must be mingled with fear. The teacher must be familiar and friendly with his pupil. He must never be sulky. To be sulky is to confess his inferiority. The instinct of the child at once perceives it, and finds its revenge in it. It therefore requires a considerable amount of good humour to teach well ; but humour combined with great decision and firmness of character. A vigorous, healthy, cheerful, jocular nature, is almost indispensable to every successful teacher, for the teacher has much to endure, without being perceived to endure it ; and if his own native disposition do not preserve almost without an effort his placidity of manner, he will find the effort too great for him, and sink under it. It seems almost miraculous to some unsuccessful teachers, how others succeed in maintaining the order and discipline so indispensable in a school ; and women, whose patience amongst children far eclipses that of men in general, not only preserve better discipline, but teach those things which they do understand better than men can teach them.

FLOGGING GIRLS.

Discursive readers of weekly and monthly journals, and especially of those organs which are addressed to the fair moiety of the public, are aware that correspondence is among their leading features. The feminine papers are usually half made up of questions and answers. One may say of their patrons, as of the people in "the days of Noe," that in these free and frank columns they "buy and sell, eat and drink, marry and are given in marriage"—for there barter-markets are established, whereby the gentle merchants exchange old music for ostrich feathers and the like; there cookery receipts by the score are requested and solicited; while the love affairs avowed and consulted upon are endless. We trust that we may be permitted, for the edification of the general public, to draw upon the treasures of a remarkable interchange of opinion appearing in this way in our amiable contemporary *The Englishwoman's Domestic Journal*. It seems that the question had arisen whether or not it was desirable and proper to flog children generally, and growing girls in particular. We are not able to state the origin of the epistolary quarrel: our attention has been arrested by the hot battle with which it closes, and from it we shall glean the amazing views which certain English parents seem to entertain respecting home discipline. As far as we can gather, "A Perplexed Mamma" began the controversy by asking what she should do with her unruly girls; and, upon this, "Pro-Rod," "A Lover of Obedience," and certain other enthusiasts for domestic flogging, warmly recommended the birch At the point of the contest where we come in, this view is ardently sustained by a phalanx of terrible mammas, sternly brandishing slippers, canes, or birch-twigs. "A Teacher of Troublesome Girls" writes: "I should strongly recommend 'A Perplexed Mother' to try the effect of a smart whipping, and I think if administered to the eldest it will very likely be beneficial to the younger ones. I do not think the slipper of much use as an instrument of punishment, unless for quite young children." "A Schoolmistress" takes the same view of the slipper as an instrument of virtue, and advocates "uncovering" the victim, and applying the punishment to a portion of the frame morally most sensitive. These connoisseurs in justice are backed by "Pater," who appears to be "baith faither and mither" in a sense of tremendous force for his hapless offspring. He says: "Two years ago I lost my wife, having two daughters, aged twelve and fourteen years, and found them completely defying control. I consulted with their aunts on the mother's side, and several medical men, upon the punishment of refractory girls and women in reformatories; all agreed that whipping in the usual manner was the best mode to adopt, and that, however severely the rod was applied, no personal injury would result, nor would the health suffer. I therefore adopted this punishment, but privately in my bedroom." To these awful "aunts on the mother's side," and this reformatory "Pater," succeeds an unabashed "Lover of the Rod," whose heart is sad because she "has observed of late years a tendency to go to a perfect idolatry of children." This gentle creature applauds Solomon's precept—forgetting, apparently, that Rehoboam turned out a particularly bad boy—and "heartily believes in the good old birch-rod." She gives her advice thus: "On the first occasion on which the girls show signs of disobedience, order all three up to the mother's bedroom, to wait until she comes. I would keep them all three in suspense, as not comprehending your intentions. Then I would provide myself either with a good birch-rod or cane (a cane is very severe), go upstairs, shut the doors, at once tell the oldest one you are going to give her a flogging. Doubtless she will feel much astonished and very indignant; but if you are firm, and threaten to call in the servant to help you, she will submit. There must be shame as well as pain in this; but she has deserved them, in my opinion; and one such punishment, in the presence of her two sisters, will do everything." But rod and slipper are despised by "Another Lover of Obedience." His method is: "When children commit an offence, I do not punish them at the time, but order them to my bedroom some few hours after. The effect of my discipline is such that they never fail to do so. When there they are laid across the bed, their clothes removed, and from fifteen to fifty smart strokes administered, the amount varying with the offence. After this I can assure you they are perfectly docile for some time to come. I have tried many systems, but find this to be the best. I should advise all to follow this same plan; they will find it answer remarkably well. Even at the age of eighteen, should my children require it, I will administer corporal chastisement." After such an inventive enthusiast for obedience, who dexterously combines suspense and agony, we must hold most reasonable the plea of another fond parent, who thinks that there is nothing wrong in slapping baby "with a satin slipper, to let it know there is a will superior to its own." This would seem the *elegantiæ* of the Art, the very æsthetics of corporal punishment —were it not for the same Mamma's declaration that she "detests the moral system." Should the baby grow up unimproved by slipper, a resource is offered her, and those like her, by yet another "Lover of Obedience," who writes: "The Editor has my address, and I hope will be kind enough to give it to any mother who may wish to send her daughters to me for a few months; I will return them obedient and good. I have never yet taken charge of young ladies, but would willingly do so to prove my theory correct."

With this ogress, panting for the screams and blood of victims whom she offers to manufacture into slaves, we close our quotations on one side. We owe it to the *Englishwoman's Journal* and Englishwomen generally, that we should set off against these abominable letters a few of the indignant protests which happily appear upon the other side Honour to the "Lady of Title" who hears with shame and a shock "the scenes that seem to go on in some houses." Several "English Mothers" express their deep indignation and shame at the correspondence on the "Pro-Rod" side.

"Gentleness" believes that such mothers and fathers "must have nigger blood in them," and have "learned in suffering what they teach in shame." "Martha" "trusts that if 'A Perplexed Mother' attempts to flog her eldest daughter the tables will be turned, and she may suffer herself; then she will know whether corporal chastisement is effectual or not" "A Christian Parent" says very rightly: "As for the 'English Mamma,' who has stated that she inflicts twenty strokes with a birch-rod upon her luckless offspring, she herself, by this admission most requires correction; and a sound scourging would be a fitting punishment for such unwomanly brutality. Patience, gentleness, and firmness are the qualities required in dealing with children and all young people; but 'like produces like,' and in each of the above cases the violent and evil passions of the child are but inherited from the father or mother. On the parents, therefore, the chief blame should rest; and to discipline *themselves* is my advice." "S. T. R." concludes that "some mothers are literally brute beasts," and does not wonder that girls arriving at womanhood escape from such dens "at any cost of self-respect." There are a few feminine professors of the Art of Domestic Education who advocate "a little, just a little, of the stick." "Trophime," for example, would always leave the clothes on if the girl be sixteen; and "Experience" uses the "rod of birch" only as a last resort. But the overwhelming number of mothers, we are glad to say, hurl contempt and anathemas at these cold-blooded "Lovers of Obedience," who thus "hate their own flesh;" and the preponderance of opinion is entirely with the "moral system" which the lady, who beats her babies with a slipper, so naturally "detests."

But what a picture of domestic misery and stupid cruelty is unveiled by the other side of this extraordinary correspondence! No wonder that girls go wrong, and throw their womanhood away in sin and anguish, when their youth is passed with fathers and mothers whose stupidity is such that they confound brutality with discipline, and are not ashamed to boast of the outrages they commit on their own flesh and blood. If we have appeared to cite the complacent suggestions of such people with patience, it was because no words of condemnation could be so severe as their own description of themselves and their ways. To those parents the great and sacred gift of children has come like pearls to swine. Perhaps in many cases it is their heads more than their hearts which are at fault, and their dense ignorance leaves them with no sense of right. But, whatever may be the cause, that which they call love of obedience is lust of power and wicked impatience; they play the tyrant over their helpless offspring, and think themselves virtuous, while they are absolutely criminal. If the secrets of all hearts were known, it would be probably seen that the parents who flogged and tortured their children for lies and evil conduct first taught them those offences by their own characters, and deserved the scourge much more thoroughly. This correspondence is a serious thing; it reveals the existence of a whole world of unnatural and indefensible private cruelty, of which law ought to have cognisance. We do not live in the Roman times, when a parent might sell a son into slavery, or take his life. These are Christian days, and each human soul has its dignity and its rights, to be respected and enforced. It would do some of these smirking malefactors good to be denounced and punished at the police-court for that which is not less "an assault with violence" because it is committed by a child's natural protector. We have all learned from Mr. Rarey that whipping is the worst way, and gentleness the best way, with horses, dogs, and the dumb creation. We have abolished flogging in the army, and it will linger only during this session in the navy. The cat is now reserved as an indescribable disgrace for garotters in gaol, and—as it seems—for the tender girl-children of many a "respectable" household. Emphatically we denounce this relic of the past generation; we say that to beat a girl-child is shameful and abominable, and never yet had any result but mischief to the victim and degradation to the executioner. As one reads these detestable confessions, there can no longer be any surprise felt that young girls "go astray," even from the home of the well-to-do classes. They "escape" from the vile discipline of the scourge like creatures maddened, without a vestige of self-respect or honour. We did not expect to find the ancient fallacy of "Virtue taught by Violence" displaying its cloven feet in so many households. For that reason it is that we have freely plagiarised from this correspondence. The brute creation is more tender and more intelligent to its young than such human sires and dams; and, indeed, avowals and advice so hideous make us recall the invocation which old HERBERT offers to the God of Love and Mercy: "With man, *of all beasts*, be not Thou a stranger!"

BIRCH-ROD QUESTION.

"A Rector" writes, "I am glad to see that the subject of the Punishment of Children is again alluded to in your 'Conversazione.' I think it was dropped too soon. Surely it is as important and interesting a subject to Englishwomen as tight-lacing or the use of a spur in riding, which has occupied more time and space than this thoroughly practical and domestic question. Although I am only in early middle life, I am 'old-fashioned' enough to regret the disuse of corporal punishment both at home and at school; and, with many others, I believe that the loss of parental authority, and the precious independence and lawlessness of young persons, are due in no small degree to this fact. No longer ago than my own childhood it was otherwise. I and my brothers were whipped, and I believe we are all the better for it. At any rate, we never doubted then or since that our good mother was right; I have never loved or respected her the less for our well-deserved punishment. Nor was the use of the rod confined to boys. I remember we used to look with a sort of awe upon a lady who lived near us, and attended the same church with a family of girls, because it was the current report that she was a very strict disciplinarian, and used the birch-rod unsparingly. Nor could I ever understand why girls should not be whipped just as much a sboys, if they deserved it. If the good old custom had not been allowed to go out, there would not have been so many 'girls of the period' at the present day. A dignitary of the Church whom I know was so convinced of this, that when he lost his wife he still occasionally used the rod himself while his daughters were still children. In former times both home governesses and schoolmistresses used the rod, both with girls and boys, as a matter of course. I could quote instances in abundance in proof of this; but '*nous avons changé tout cela,*' and changed for the worse, too. The birch is happily still used at all the older grammar-schools for boys, but I fear that in girls' schools it is seldom heard of—at least, I should be very glad to hear it if your correspondents can report otherwise. I remember, some fifteen years ago, a boy told it me as a rather wonderful thing that at the school where his sister was 'they birched the girls just like boys.' Whether they do so still I do not know. I shall be glad to say a few words more on this topic on a future occasion."

"Tiny" agrees with the remarks made by "An English Lady" on the Birch-rod question. There is something in it perfectly revolting to any refined female mind. If children are properly brought up, with a clear knowledge of right and wrong, their education being based upon sound religious teaching, depend upon it at fifteen years of age they will not require such a degrading punishment. "Tiny" is a mother, and she would never punish her child in any such way, and were she positively compelled to do so the pain and grief to herself would be far greater than any the child would feel; and most certainly "Tiny" would never boast of the punishment as "A Mother" does. Children are gifted with reasoning powers, and should be taught that their first duty is strict obedience—the unquestioning obedience which is cheerfully given, because they know no one can have their welfare so much at heart as their parents. And mothers should so act as to win the respect of their children How can an intelligent girl of fifteen respect the mother who chastises her as she would an unruly spaniel? Where such correction is needed, depend upon it the bringing up of the child is at fault. Teach a child that her mother is her best friend, enter into all her childish pleasures and sorrows, and at fifteen she will be a companion, not a plague. "Tiny" wishes that all mothers (and fathers) would remember that there is a never-ending life when this is at an end, and by so acting themselves teach their children to reflect that the eye of God is ever upon them, beholding all they do, and by education of this kind they will be a blessing in after years to all around them. Why have we the "girls of the period," of whom all sensible people make fun? Because their mind has not been carefully cultivated in their childhood. Should they have the blessing to be under the care of a religious governess, the good she does is speedily obliterated from the mind by the conduct of the fashionable mother of the day. May the days soon come when Englishwomen will learn to act as "seeing Him who is invisible," and then they will deeply repent the neglect or harsh usage of their children, and be heartily ashamed of their false hair and teeth, made-up complexions, peg-top heels, &c., and the time and money uselessly spent which ought to be devoted to the service of God and welfare of their fellow-creatures! Perhaps "Tiny" is somewhat severe in her remarks, but she so deeply deplores the state of Englishwomen of the period, especially amongst the aristocracy, that she is obliged to say all she thinks.

"A Scotch Mother" (Dundee) says: "It appears from the letters in your Magazine that some correspondent wishes further information on the subject of Whipping Children. Now, before the subject closes, I would be much obliged to any of your lady correspondents who would give me information through your columns on the following points:—Whether a whipping has more good effect on boys than girls—that is to say, which requires the rod to be used most seldom; and also at what age can boys be whipped by ladies, my opinion being that except at a very early age few ladies can inflict a chastisement on boys sufficiently severe to be long remembered."

In regard to the Proper Chastisement of the Young, "Agnes M." writes:—"While you have so many opinions expressed, both for and against corporal punishment for girls, perhaps the opinion of one who has herself suffered during her youth may be acceptable. Up to the age of sixteen I was educated at home, and I believe to a certain extent spoiled; on arriving at that age I was placed at a finishing school near Bath, in the charge of a lady who was dearly loved by all her pupils, but at the same time did not fail to punish them severely for their faults. At the same time I had a very bad habit of boastful fibbing—a habit which she reprimanded very sternly soon after I was placed there; this not having the desired effect, she one morning sent for me to her sitting-room, and there told me of her intention of endeavouring to effect a cure of this habit by inflicting a whipping. I was then sent to my bedroom in charge of a governess, to remove my underclothing, and on my return to the sitting-room, was obliged to lie across an ottoman, while the punishment was inflicted with a birchen-rod. I was somewhat resentful at the time, but have since had much cause to be grateful, for two or three similar applications quite cured me. This is now eight years ago, and should I ever have any daughters, I should not hesitate to treat them in a like manner."

"The husband of a Schoolmistress" writes: "My wife keeps a boarding-school for little girls. The youngest is just turned six; the eldest about twelve. One of the pupils, just turned nine, was detected in a moral offence. My wife took her into a private room alone and inflicted, *more materno*, a chastisement with a rod. The mother called the following day, was indignant, and removed the child. I claimed a quarter's payment, in lieu of notice. This was peremptorily refused. It was agreed that the question should be referred to a neighbouring magistrate, a retired barrister with a family of daughters. He heard the child's statement and that of the mother as to the marks on the child's person, &c. When they had finished he asked my wife whether she had been in the habit of so punishing her scholars; to which she answered in the affirmative. He then said that he did not wish to hear anything more from her, that his own children were so corrected, and that the quarter's payment in lieu of notice must be paid."

"A Rector" writes: "It would be a difficult task to enumerate the numberless authorities in favour of corporal punishment for children from Solomon to our own day. Some of the greatest names would be contained in the List. Thus Dr. Arnold always defended and advocated this form of discipline, and practised it himself. The head-master of another large public school, in his evidence before the Royal Commission, not only declared it was the wisest and most efficacious form of punishment, but said it had a good effect upon the body and mind of children—it quickens the circulation of the blood, and is, therefore, specially beneficial to children of sluggish temperament and dull understanding. I believe he quoted the opinion of medical men in support of this. It has a good effect also as teaching that sin brings pain. It is nonsense to talk of reasoning with children. Authority is what they require. Reason will come in due time. But the first duty of the parent is to secure obedience. Many parents are evidently most unfit for their responsible position, and have no right to be parents, and will only bring up undisciplined children who will cause misery to themselves and others. Many of your correspondents are evidently of this class of ignorant and silly parents. If children are properly brought up, the use of the rod will become less frequent as they grow older, till it will be altogether laid aside, and a word, a look, or a remonstrance will be enough. Many children nothing but pain will subdue; passionate children, sulky and obstinate children, and those addicted to falsehood and idleness, are such. A prompt and *severe* whipping will do what hours of reasoning or pleading will not effect, and this is better for the child and the parent too. There is no punishment that girls and boys dread so much as a whipping. It is a real punishment and a personal one, while many of the substitutes for it are unequal, unfair, injurious, and ineffective.

"A Schoolmistress" writes: "Sir, I am rejoiced to see that the subject of the Personal Chastisement of Children is again being brought forward. Now no one has tested the exceeding efficacy of a systematic use of the rod more than I have done, so I gladly give my experience—extending now over thirty-five years. Up to twelve years of age I was brought up by my aunt, who kept up my father's house (my mother died when I was very young). During this time no attempt was made to correct by physical pain (except of the mildest description) my many evil propensities and bad habits; but after I was twelve, my father married again, and I was sent to a boarding-school in Norwich, where, when I had been about three weeks, I had my first whipping. I had been guilty of gross misconduct, and told a lie to screen myself. And the punishment inflicted on me was the beginning of my entire reformation. I shall never forget that first whipping, how I was told after prayers to go to Mrs. S.'s private sitting-room; how, after a most loving reprimand, I was told that as reproof had failed to do me good, I must prepare to be whipped; Mrs. S. then rang the bell, and giving to the maid who answered it a long woollen dress, which she took from a hanging closet, bade her see that I put that on and came back to her. The maid, an old confidential servant, took me into Mrs. S.'s bedroom, made me undress, and don the long woollen garment, which fastened round the waist with a band and was open down each side from the waist to the feet. I then was bidden to put my feet in a pair of list slippers. This being done, the maid, carrying off all my clothes to my own bedroom, requested me to go back to the room where I had left Mrs. S., and give four knocks at the door. Instead of doing this, I lingered in the passage, where the maid found me a few minutes afterwards. She said, 'You must follow me.' I did so, and she remained till I had knocked four times at the door. On being told to enter, I found Mrs. S sitting at a table reading, but on the table lay a long, lithe birch-rod; pushing the table on one side, Mrs S., taking up the rod, pointed to a long narrow stool, which I afterwards knew as 'the horse,' and told me to lie across it. The previous preparation, and Mrs. S.'s manner, so awed me that I submitted. I then found myself buckled across by a strap across the horse. I heard Mrs. S. fasten the door and draw a heavy curtain across it. She then very quickly folded the back part of the woollen dress—which was loose on each side from the waist to the feet—above my waist; then very briefly speaking of my faults, she grasped the rod, and gave me very deliberately a most severe birching. Of course I screamed, and shrieked, and implored, but the rod pursued its destined course, and wielded by Mrs. S.'s strong arm, it did its destined work. The stinging pain, the after-feeling and marks, the present shame, the necessary submission, the ceremony observed—all did their work; and as I took my course to bed, I felt the first overthrow of the old

A.Z

rebellious nature. From that time till I was sixteen I had to pay seven similar visits to Mrs. S. in that same private room, and to go through even more severe whippings. But behold the fruit. At nineteen I became a teacher in the same school; I remained for ten years Mrs. S.'s much-trusted assistant. I have now for very many years had a school of my own, and I myself administered corporal punishment with the birch-rod in precisely the same way as I have described my first whipping, and we have never known it to fail. By 'we' I mean Mrs. S., myself, my teachers, the parents of my pupils; and dozens of pupils, in their happy after lives, have, in most grateful terms, thanked me for my discipline. I am most anxious that this should be made public, and shall gladly furnish many special cases, and give any information."

"A Rejoicer in the Restoration of the Rod" says: "I call myself by this title because I do most firmly believe that a great many of the acknowledged evils of the present age—undutiful children, and reckless, heedless young men and women—arise from so many parents and teachers having of late years neglected a most essential duty in not using sufficient and proper corporal chastisement. But from all I hear a great reaction is taking place in this respect. And though there may be many loving mothers, like 'Tiny,' who shrink from it, yet I rejoice that true love is being more shown in duty triumphing over sentiment, and that the rod—the birch-rod—is regaining its old place both among boys and girls; so much so that I believe it is a very rare thing to find a preparatory school for boys—especially those conducted by ladies—where the rod is not more or less used. I know one most excellent school of this kind in Kentish Town, London, where there are boys from six to fourteen, and where the very kind and good ladies who manage it (and who have always more applications for admission than they can receive) administer the rod in a way which, if 'A Scotch Mother' could witness, would effectually negative her idea of ladies not being able to birch a boy worth mentioning after he ceased to be a little boy."

"Florence" (Oakley Square) thus narrates her experience : "Both my brother and myself were spoiled, in the fullest sense of the word. My father spoiled me, and my mother spoiled my brother. However, when I was fourteen years of age my parents were compelled to go abroad for mamma's health, and I was left under the guardianship of a maiden aunt, who quickly decided that a strict school was the best place for me. To a school in Hertfordshire I was accordingly sent, the schoolmistress having been previously informed that I was 'a child of wayward disposition.' I had not been there a week before 'the spirit of opposition which pervaded me,' as my aunt used to term it, got me into hot water, and I was ordered to bed. I had not been undressed many minutes, when Miss Margaret, one of the principals, came into the bedroom, and after well lecturing me on my conduct, told me she intended to whip me. She then rang the bell, and one of the maids brought a birch-rod, and I was told to prepare, which I flatly refused to do. As I was rebellious, the maid tied my hands together with a towel, the end of which she fastened to a peg high up on the wall, so that I could only just reach the floor with the tips of my toes. Miss Margaret then gave me a severe flogging, Finding I was obstinate, after a minute or two she desisted and left the room, leaving me with the maid. I tried hard to get off the peg, but could not. When Miss Margaret returned she asked me whether I was sorry. 'No!' I shouted. 'Then I must whip you again,' she said, suiting the action to the word. This second whipping was too much for my spirit, and I begged for forgiveness. The rest of the day I did not cease crying, not so much from the pain as from mortification that I had met my match and been conquered. Strange as it may seem, from that day to the present I have loved Miss Margaret, and felt her to be a true friend. As I believe great benefit has resulted from corporal punishment, I think it right to advocate it, for I know from observation that if our faults are not corrected when we are young, we generally suffer in a far harder school when we grow up."

"Mrs. L. Gray" writes: "Being a mother of three daughters, the eldest being thirteen and the youngest nine years old, who have, up to the present time, given me great trouble in managing, I have determined, since reading the letters in your last number signed 'Agnes M.' and 'A Schoolmistress,' as a last resource, to whip them. I am sure many of your subscribers and myself would feel greatly obliged to the lady who signed herself 'A Schoolmistress' if she would kindly give us a few instances where whipping has proved effective, and if she or any of your readers will inform me how old I may pursue that course of correction, as I have had a niece put under my care whose parents are in India, who is very wilful and disobedient, and, being nearly sixteen, I do not know how to punish her without whipping her. I should feel greatly obliged to any of your readers who would kindly let me know through your valuable Magazine of a shop where I could get good birch-rods from in London, as I am going to reside there in future. I am sure you would be conferring a boon upon parents if you would publish the many letters that have appeared upon the chastisement of children, when the correspondence closes, in a separate book."

From Philadelphia, U.S, "A Sister" writes: "I have seen a subject discussed in your magazine which at this present time is very interesting to me. I refer to the personal chastisement of children. My case is this. I have my two younger sisters to bring up (their mother being dead), and I find great difficulty in making them obey. They are often extremely disobedient and naughty. The only punishment that I have yet inflicted upon them is a box on the ears, or sending them to bed, neither of which I find does them any good. Their father has given me full control over them, and says if I find it well to whip them to do so; but I would first like to ask some elder sister who has had the bringing up of some younger ones if it is well for a sister to administer corporal punishment? I see none of the letters in your Magazine are from sisters, or I would not have troubled you with this. I see most of your correspondents advocate a bunch of twigs as the best instrument of correction. I should like to ask if they leave any marks for any length of time, when applied without covering; because I do not wish to be too severe, although I should like the punishment to be effectual. By inserting this as soon as possible you will greatly oblige."

A lady, signing "Experience," writes: "As many of your readers seem anxious to know how to punish girls of fifteen years old and upwards, I take the liberty of informing you that about three years ago my eldest girl gave me a good deal of trouble by disregarding my directions and orders. She was then turned sixteen, was home from school for her holidays, and evidently thought that under those circumstances she was entitled to do just what she pleased. I spoke to her three or four times very seriously, and at last threatened that if she continued to disregard what I said to her I should be compelled to enforce my orders with the birch. When my children were little I had been used, if they were naughty, to lay them across my knee and whip them with my slipper or a small birch-rod, but now this mode of procedure was not available, as my daughter was too big for that treatment, and would only laugh at the slight pats she would receive. It being a real struggle for the mastery, it was important that my authority should be strongly supported, and if it were not for this I do not think that I should have whipped her at all. What I did was this: I bought a birch-broom, and took from it twenty long, stiff, and bushy switches, tied them together with string, the handle being about as thick as my wrist. Shortly after it was made I had occasion to use it. I first lectured the culprit, and then pinioned her arms behind her back, laid her across a sofa, and applied the birch sharply. She promised amendment, and I left off, telling her at the same time that I would whip her again if she broke her word. Before a week was over she had done so, and I was afraid that what I had done was useless, perhaps worse. However, I determined to give it another trial. I did so, this time making her first remove her drawers.

I gave her twenty strokes deliberately, and with excellent effect, for since she has conducted herself well, and I have not had to repeat the experiment of birch-rod. My advice to mothers is this: Do not use the rod unless you are absolutely obliged, but if you do use it make it smartly felt. It is no disgrace to a girl to be whipped by her mother—the disgrace is deserving it. Boys of the very highest birth are constantly flogged by their fathers and masters, and why should not a girl be whipped by her mother or governess?"

"G. H. D." (Greenwich) writes: "I see that the subject of whipping children is revived in the columns of your journal, and as it is a most important question I beg to suggest a few thoughts concerning it. First, I would ask, Are the ideas of your 'whipping correspondents' with regard to the treatment of children, and especially the degradation of the birch-rod, consistent with the following words of our Saviour and St. Paul, or do they not rather spring from parental arrogance? Jesus said, 'Suffer little *children* to come unto me, and forbid them not, for of *such* is the kingdom of heaven.' And again, 'Except *ye* be born again, and become as a little *child*, ye cannot enter into the kingdom of heaven.' Our Lord here sets up children as examples to such conceited parents and adults who despise them because they are *children*, innocent and weak. St. Paul says, 'Be ye followers of God, as dear *children*;' and again he says a bishop should be 'one that ruleth well his own house,' but '*no striker*.' Solomon has been quoted as an authority for the rod, but Jesus has said, 'A greater than Solomon is here'; and Solomon and his son Rehoboam are bad *examples* of life, whatever his *precepts* may have been to the Jews. Again, we cannot be Christians and Jews at the same time; and if we whip the children we must stone the adulteress, &c.; but Jesus said, 'Let him that is without sin among you first cast a stone at her.' And as it is undoubtedly true that 'the violent and evil passions of the child are inherited from the parents,' let us first remove the beam from our own eye, and then we shall see clearly to remove the mote from our children's eyes. I especially entreat the attention of your correspondent, 'A Rector,' to the foregoing quotations from Holy Scripture. I think the picture of a clergyman administering the Blessed Sacrament with a birch-rod dangling from his girdle is very inconsistent. 'A Scotch mother' asks, 'At what age can boys be whipped by ladies?' This question might be paraphrased unpleasantly. I would ask some of the 'lovers of the rod,' How would you manage disobedient wives and second childhood? Your correspondent 'Tiny,' on the birch-rod system, says truly, 'There is something in it perfectly revolting to any refined female mind.' She might have said 'male or female' with equal truth; and I am indeed surprised and ashamed at the opinions of some ladies on this subject. I cannot understand how persons holding such brutal principles can call themselves gentle-men and gentle-women. I would earnestly call your readers' attention to a most interesting article in *Good Words* for the month of January, entitled, 'The French Reformatory of St. Michael, Paris.' There they will read of *complete* success without punishment of any kind, and that under trying circumstances. Surely if this be possible on so large a scale, and between strangers, it is easy of accomplishment at home, where the *mother* has direct influence over the child from the earliest hours of its existence. Finally, let us remember that while St. Paul enjoins obedience on children, he also says, 'Ye *fathers* provoke not your children to wrath.'"

"Alice de V." (Kensington) writes: "Surely if the letters upon Chastising Children are real, they cannot be written by *ladies*, but must come from those who are

"'Born in the garret—in the kitchen bred,'

'whose 'usban's keep 'orses, and 'unt the 'ounds three times hevery week.' No wonder we hear such things of the 'girls of the period,' when there are such mammas in the world! Why do they not civilise themselves, correct their own evil dispositions, and set a good example to their children, instead of chastising them for merely being small editions of their coarse-minded mammas? I am confident that whipping girls degrades them, and takes away every feeling of self-respect and modesty. I think the letter from 'A Schoolmistress' conclusively proves this. I was much pleased with the Virginian lady's letter. I wish she would give us her opinion of the 'mammas of the period.'"

THE TRUE STORY OF FATHER GIRARD AND MISS CADIERE.

One day Girard informed his penitent that she was to be favoured by a remarkable vision, during which she would (by spiritual agency) be drawn up into the air, he alone, as her spiritual Father, would be permitted to witness this manifestation; but Miss Cadiere, at the appointed time, was not in a willing mood, in spite of the Holy man's threats and entreaties. She resisted the spiritual influence, held fast hold of her chair, and would not permit herself to be drawn up. Finding his expostulations useless, the Father quitted the room in a rage, and sent Guiol to rebuke his pupil. Although Miss Cadiere, when in a calmer mood the same evening, asked pardon and promised future obedience, Father Girard determined that her crime should be expiated by a heavy penance. The next morning, accordingly, he visited her, and flourishing "a discipline," he said, "God demands, in His justice, that you, having refused to allow yourself to be invested with His gifts, should now, in punishment for your sins, undress yourself and be chastised. Truly have you deserved that the whole Earth should witness this infliction on you; but God has graciously permitted that only I and this wall (which cannot speak) should be witnesses of your shame. But beforehand, swear to me an oath of fidelity, for both you and I would be plunged into ruin if the secret was discovered." Girard had his desire, Miss Cadiere humbly submitted to discipline, and the scene which followed we must leave the reader to imagine.

THE KNOUT APPLIED TO AN EMPRESS.

When the Empress Eudoxia was sentenced by her husband, Peter the Great, to undergo the Punishment of the Knout on a charge of infidelity, she no sooner saw the dreadful apparatus than, to avoid torture, she readily confessed every species of criminality they were inclined to lay to her charge. She owned every amorous intrigue with which she was accused, and of which, to all appearance, till that horrible moment she never had the least idea. Eudoxia was, however, condemned to undergo the discipline, which was administered in full chapter, by the hands of two ecclesiastics.

KING OF FIJI AND HIS WIVES.

In a recent work on Fiji and the Fijians is a graphic account of the Marriage Ceremony or Contract as observed in this savage region. The misery of the woman begins directly after the ceremony. If she be young and pretty the old big-fisted wives turn their venom against her, and do all they can, by mauling and ill-treatment, to render her as unsightly as themselves. If she be of the brawny sort, as well able to give as to take a thrashing, then she is hated, and all sorts of secret means are used to work her ruin. As may be easily imagined, these domestic brawls occasionally interfere with the peace of the lord of the establishment. What does the despotic husband do on such emergencies? Does he go out and reason with the brawlers? Does he use gentle persuasion, to make them desist from this biting and scratching? No; he has by him a stout stick kept for the purpose, and rushing amongst his women he lays about him till order is restored.

The staff used by the King for this purpose was inlaid with ivory, but did not on that account give less pain.

PUNISHMENT OF THE KNOUT IN RUSSIA.

Olearius gives a description of the manner in which he saw the knout inflicted on eight men and one woman, only for selling brandy and tobacco without a licence. The executioner's man, after stripping them down to the waist, tied their feet, and took one at a time on his back. The executioner stood at three paces distant with a large pizzle, to the end of which were fastened three thongs of an elk's skin, untanned, with which, springing forward, whenever he struck, the blood gushed out at every blow.

After their backs were thus dreadfully mangled, they were whipped through the City of Petersburg for about a mile and a-half, and then dismissed.

SCOURGING.

On page 247 of the American work Obliviad, occurs the following on Mistaken Words, which "comes from youths not having been often enough scourged at school; where, indeed, in former times, boys were ashamed of such improprieties, and needed no other punishment thán the fool's-cap. The business of flogging has thus doubled on the Satyrist, when it is too late, and age has made Carlyles incorrigible. Birch must drop again with blood, though it be patrician, and the horse be kept in Eton, before boys, and men, write readable English. The unflogged of the *New Œtonian* has sent in the following as a specimen :—'We do not mean to imply that there is anything very vicious or degrading in the casual enjoyment of desultory refreshment. Far from it.'—'Really,' writes our friend of the *Athenæum*, 'if this be the best Eton can do, Eton must have fallen sadly off. Compare this stuff with the *Old Œtonian*, and the difference is the difference between childishness and manliness. A straining upon the facetious which is not comic, and an occasional grandiloquence which is anything but impressive." The *Athenæum*, I am afraid, needs the rod, as much as the boy: the difference is the difference between childishness and manliness: anything but impressive.

WIFE BEATING.

The wife of an old negro on the neighbouring estate of Anchovy had lately forsaken him for a younger lover. One night when she happened to be alone, the incensed husband entered her hut unexpectedly, abused her with all the rage of jealousy, and demanded the clothes to be restored, which he had formerly given her. On her refusal he drew a knife, and threatened to cut them off her back; nor could she persuade him to depart until she had received a severe beating at his hands.—*Monk Lewis Journal.*

THE FLAGELLATING MONKS AND THE BEAR.

At Lent time, when religious fraternities are accustomed to inflict on themselves certain discipline, there was in a certain Italian city a confraternity of Penitents. A pastrycook in the same city had a tame bear, which ran about the streets, doing no harm to anyone. Wandering about one evening, it found its way into the chapel (the door of which stood open), coiled itself up in a corner and went to sleep. When the penitents were all assembled, the door was locked, and after a short exhortation from the altar, they spread themselves about the chapel. The light was hidden behind a pillar; the most zealous commenced by inflicting punishment on themselves; an example that was soon followed. The noise woke up the bear, who, in trying to make his way out, stumbled against the penitents, who, with their breeches down, were inflicting castigations.

A.Z.

The bear felt with his paw to find what it was; from one behind he passed on quietly to another; and the penitents in their fear, began to think it was the devil who had come there to disturb them in their devotions. Their suspicions became a certainty, when the bear passing by the pillar where the light was, they saw his shadow on the wall. It was who should get to the door first! And to this day nothing would convince these worthy disciplinarians that they had not received a visit from the arch-fiend in person.

A CONJUGAL SCENE.

"Let you go, my angel! What, just as I have recovered my lost treasure! No! let them come in and see how naughty children are punished when they rebel against lawful authority."

So saying he came tripping across the room as he spoke, and flung the door open, admitting into a somewhat odd scene. Fifine was tied across a heavy chair in the middle of the room, crying as if her heart would break, her clothes turned up with the utmost precision, while the ugliest old man I ever saw was administering a whipping, which had already been severe, judging from the state of her hips and her tear-stained and swollen face.

"Pardon, ladies," he said with an odious leer, "Shall not a man do what he likes with his own? This lady is my runaway wife, my chattel, my goods: and who shall forbid my chastising her when I find her."—*St. Bridget.*

FANCIFUL FLOGGING.

She got hold of a book out of the library about the feminine customs of Rome, and she resolved to make me attend upon her toilet as the slaves of the Roman ladies did. So she looked up a short tunic which was among the fancy dresses, and the next morning she made me go and strip, and come back to her with nothing on but this garment, which was just like a sack, with short sleeves only, of soft white merino, trimmed with red satin. It did not come to my knees, and my legs and feet were bare, except for a pair of sandals of red leather.

"Now take care what you are about, Perkins," she said, "I am going to deal with you exactly as the ladies in Rome dealt with their slaves."

"But I am not a slave, my lady," I said, pertinently enough, I dare say, for I felt angry. "There are no slaves here."

"You are mine as long as you are in my room," she replied, "When my toilet is sufficiently completed I shall punish you for that speech." She made me bathe her, and dress her hair, and then before she put on her stays she said quite calmly, "Bring the rod." I brought it, and she made me kneel and kiss her, and beg her pardon for what I had said; and then I knelt on the couch, and she whipped me till she was tired,—and I,—well, I did not get over it for a long time.

Merry Order.

REVELATIONS OF BOARDING-SCHOOL PRACTICES.

At the age of seventeen I was sent to a fashionable boarding-school, near Exeter, in Devonshire. I was sent there owing to the influence of my aunt, who was always praising this establishment up to my mamma, and strongly recommending it as a finishing academy for young ladies. My aunt was a maiden lady of forty, a fine, tall, handsome, buxom woman.

Neither myself nor my mamma ever thought she was an advocate for the rod, and liked administering, and seeing it administered. It turned out afterwards, as the narrative will show, that she was really in league with the schoolmistress, and would frequently call at the establishment and indulge herself in her favourite pastime, for which she no doubt paid large sums annually, being a strong and fervent advocate for corporal chastisement, at times an unseen observer and with some of the elder young ladies being the operator. In all there were twenty-four young ladies in this fashionable establishment, their ages varying from twelve to nineteen. I was as tall, fine-shaped, and handsome as any young lady in the school, and no doubt when my mamma gave her consent to my leaving home, my aunt thought there was a great treat in store for her.

A few days after arriving, I soon found out what sort of lady principal I had to contend with, and her assistants were not much better. The first sample I saw her administer to one of her pupils was after I had been there four days. A young lady, about fifteen, had committed some trifling error, for which madam told her in plain terms that she should give her a good whipping when class was over, and this she did and in front of the whole school. She was taken by the arms and legs by two of the assistant teachers, and thrown face downwards over a desk sloping each way, and firmly held there. Madam then approached with a flat piece of wood about an inch-and-a-half in thickness, and shaped like a hair-brush, but much bigger. After addressing a few words of advice to us, and admonishing the culprit, she took hold of her garments at the bottom, then without any further to-do, she lifted the "spanker," as this piece of wood was called by my schoolfellows, and inflicted a tremendous "spank" across the girl. A loud yell followed, and a strong effort to free herself from the grasp of her tormentors, but all of no avail, for they, no doubt owing to their previous experience, could hold a young lady in any position. She received about a dozen stripes before she was released.

We had a system of making so many marks, and if any young lady had not made so many by the end of the week they were sure to receive a whipping. I have known as many as seven young ladies whipped on a Saturday. It was at these whippings that my aunt and her friends were present as unseen spectators, through the medium of small glass panels being inserted in a door to an adjoining closet.

In fact, during my two years at this establishment I was whipped several times. I shall never forget my last experience. I think the lady principal had made up her mind that I should be flogged on the Saturday, for at the early part of the week, however good I did my lessons, fault was found with me, and I got careless towards the latter end. On the Saturday I found my name on the "Black List," as it was called. I was number three on the list, my two schoolfellows, both young girls about fourteen, had gone in and received their portion, and, as usual, had been dismissed to bed after their punishment. I was then ordered in. I need not tell you that I entered the room trembling from head to foot. Madam called me by my Christian name "Emily," and informed me she was very sorry to have to inflict punishment on such a big girl as me, but the rules of the school must be enforced, winding up by ordering me to prepare for punishment. I dropped on my knees in front of her, and begged of her to take into consideration my age, size, etc.; in fact I hardly remember what I did say. She was inexorable, and, with a smile on her face, ordered me to obey, or she should have to call assistance, and my punishment would be much more severe. I made some remark, when she seized me by my beautiful long hair, and beat me about my ears, head, cheeks, and arms, with the birch, until I was compelled to give in and promise obedience in future.

Soon after I found means to send a letter to my mother, informing her of the circumstances related above. She accordingly took steps for my early removal, and I was soon afterwards married, but my mother and aunt have never been friends or spoken to each other since.

FLOGGINGS AT SEA.

However the arbitrary disposition and impetuous temper of Governor Wall may have been attenuated by years and reflection, the following anecdote, which the writer had from an eye-witness, has served to show, that Governor Wall, in the infancy of his appointment, evinced a species of vigour competent to deter mutiny, even in a part more desperate than Goree. This garrison, so desperate in name, was every way orderly; and during the kind and humane command of Capt. Lacey, flogging was abolished altogether, on the remonstrance of the surgeon; stopping their grog was found more than sufficient to check all their irregularities

Amongst the recruits consigned to his command on his passage outwards, was an unfortunate man named Green, who formerly kept a hatter's shop, in Catherine Street, Strand, and who, under a conviction for some crime, was sentenced to transportation for fourteen years. His wife, an amiable, but heart-broken woman, was permitted to accompany him on the voyage; and shortly after the vessel had sailed from the Downs, symptoms of mutiny were discovered amongst the convicts: several had sawed off their irons; and Green was charged, not with any act of mutiny, but with furnishing the convicts with money to procure the implements for taking off their irons. The unfortunate man stated in his vindication, that he had only lent some of the wretches a few shillings to take some sheets and other necessaries out of pawn. But his defence would not do. He was brought to the gangway by order of the Governor, without drum-head, or any other court-martial, and flogged with a boatswain's cat, until his bones were denuded of flesh. Still the unfortunate man never uttered a groan. The Governor, who superintended the punishment, swore he would conquer the rascal's stubbornness, and make him cry out, or whip his guts out. The surgeon remonstrated on the danger of the man's death, but in vain. Ensign Wall, the Governor's brother, a humane young man, on his knees entreated that the flogging should cease; but also in vain; and his importunity only served to provoke a threat of putting himself in arrest. He then entreated the unfortunate Green to cry out, and save himself. But the unhappy man said it was now too late, as he felt himself dying, and unable to cry out; that he had not avoided it from stubbornness, but concealed his pangs, lest his wretched wife, who was down below, and knew nothing of his situation, should hear his cries, and die with anguish. The flogging was continued until the convulsions of his bowels appeared through his lacerated loins, when he fainted under the lash, and was consigned to the surgeon, who appeared at the trial.

This event stamped a melancholy horror on the mind of the Governor's brother, that was not abated during the voyage; and on his arrival at Goree, he was seized with a raging fever, in which he died; expressing horror and execration at the cruelty of his brother (and warning the officers to beware of him), whom he would not permit to come within his sight.

The unfortunate man, notwithstanding a survival of twenty years, in the course of which it has been proved that his conduct and principles bore every mark of amendment that could atone to Society for acts committed in the pride of power, and heat of an impetuous and despotic temper; yet furnished, in his old age, an awful, but dignified illustration of the equal and impartial justice of British laws. And British subjects not only in England but in the remote and secluded region of an African island may proudly exult in the protection of those laws, and the exemplary punishment of those, who, at any distance of time, shall be convicted of violating them by wanton cruelty.

THE WHIPPING WIDOW.

It is not so very long ago, when there suddenly appeared in society, a rich, or apparently rich, widow, Mrs. W. She lived in good style, kept her carriage, and had a handsomely appointed house, and plenty of well-trained servants. No one knew the source of her wealth, or where she came from, but she rapidly became popular in the best society, and by her dashing manner and splendid appearance won for herself an eminent position in the fashionable world. Like many fine ladies, she cherished a secret passion for the rod, and odd stories began to circulate, through the medium of her maids, of the way she used it on herself and them, and report says she was accustomed to use the rod upon her late husband very freely. After his death she became acquainted with a young student, who used to visit her home on pretence of giving lessons, but in reality it was to receive a good whipping from her hands.

MIRACULOUS CURE BY THE BIRCH.

Father Nicolo, of Narni, was a celebrated preacher, and had generally a quick eye in the pulpit over the female part of his audience. He was one day preaching at Catanea in Sicily, when among the rest of his auditory, he espied out a very agreeable young woman, named Agatha, wife to one Ruggieri, a physician, and was immediately enamoured with her beauty. The lady was so devout, as to have her eye constantly fixed on the preacher, and could not help perceiving that he was handsome, nor wishing secretly that her husband were no less agreeable. After sermon she addressed herself to Father Nicolo for Confession, who was overjoyed at this lucky opportunity of discovering his passion. Agatha had soon despatched the account of her own sins; after which she very generously confessed for her husband too, and asked the holy man, if he had no cure for an old man's jealousy. The Father replied that jealousy was a passion not to be avoided, by the happy person who possessed so divine a creature. Agatha smiled, and thinking it time to return to some female friends who were waiting for her, desired Absolution. The Confessor sighed, My fair daughter, says he, who can free another that is bound himself; I am chained by the irresistible power of your beauty; and without your assistance I can neither absolve myself nor you. Agatha was young and inexperienced, yet by the help of a good natural apprehension she was not at a loss to unravel the meaning of these words. She had besides, to quicken her wit, been strictly guarded and ill-used by Doctor Ruggieri. She therefore soon let the Father see that she understood him, and that she was not displeased to find, notwithstanding the sanctity of his character, that he was flesh and blood. The business of the Absolution was not forgot: Father Nicolo pressed his passion; and at his earnest request, the lady undertook to find means that he should make her a visit. After a short pause, she acquainted him, in order to this, that she was troubled with fits, and that all the medicines her husband could administer, procured her no ease; therefore, said she, the next time he is sent for into the country, I will feign myself seized with my usual distemper, and send to you to bring some relic of St. Griffon for my relief. You will, I suppose, comply with the summons, and one of my faithful maids shall be ready to conduct you to my chamber. The Father applauded her wit, pronounced a thousand blessings on her for this happy invention, and thus they parted.

Honest Ruggieri, who dreamt nothing of what had passed, went very opportunely out of town the next morning. The lady was immediately seized with a terrible fit, and in the midst of her attendants, who were officious in helping her, frequently called on the name of St. Griffon, for assistance. The crafty confidant that stood by, and was instructed with the secret, took the hint, and pressed her to send for the relics of that saint, which she said were famous for their miraculous virtue and wonderful cures. The mistress, who seemed scarce able to utter her words, bid her do as she thought fit. Father Nicolo presently had notice, and obeyed the summons with the utmost expedition.

The Father now arrived, and followed his female guide, entered the room where the afflicted lady lay, and drew near her bedside with a becoming gravity. Agatha received him with profound reverence, and begged the charity of his prevailing prayers to Heaven, and to St. Griffon. He exhorted her to prepare herself, that she might be qualified to receive the benefit of the sacred relics and birch he had brought; in order to which, says he, it is first necessary that with a contrite heart you have recourse to Confession, that your soul being healed, your body may more easily be cured. The lady replied, she desired nothing more. This was a signal to the rest who were in the room to depart, which they presently obeyed, and left the two lovers to their private devotion.

The good Father had not long applied the birch and other relics of St. Griffon for the recovery of the devout Agatha, when Ruggieri was discovered at the entrance of the street, who returned sooner than he was either desired or expected. The lovers were immediately alarmed, and the Friar leaped upon the floor in such a fright that he forgot to take his breeches, which upon that occasion he had thrown by, as an unnecessary garment, at the bed's head.

The wench who was in the secret, opened the door, and crying out that by the favour of Heaven and of St. Griffon, her lady was almost recovered, called in the rest of the attendants. Ruggieri arrived at the same instant, but was not well pleased to observe, that a Friar had found the way to his house; nor was he less disturbed at this new illness of his wife. Agatha perceived his disorder by the change of his countenance, and immediately told him, that she had been infinitely obliged to that holy Father, by whose prayers, together with the application of the rod of St. Griffon, she had been snatched from the grave. The good man was overjoyed to hear it was no worse, and correcting himself in his own thoughts for his former suspicions, very heartily thanked the Friar, who after some pious discourse was glad to withdraw.

Father Nicolo was not gone far before he recovered out of his fright, and the same moment perceived he had left his breeches behind him. This put him into a new concern; he dared not go back, but comforted himself as well as he could in the hope that Agatha or her maid would find them first, and take care to prevent further mischief. Honest Ruggieri was now sitting on the bedside by his wife, and saying a thousand kind things to her, when unluckily putting his hand to adjust the pillow under her head, he laid hold on one of the strings, and drew out the breeches. This threw him into a worse fit than any his wife was accustomed to fall into; he stormed like a madman, and asked how that appurtenance of the Friar came there? Agatha, who had all her wits awakened by her new amour, replied, without the least hesitation, that it was what she had told him of. It is to this, says she, I owe my cure. This is the miraculous garment of St. Griffon, which the holy Father brought, and he has left it here for my greater security, till the evening, at which time he will send for it, or fetch it himself.

Poor Ruggieri, hearing so ready and unexpected an answer, believed, or pretended to believe her, and retired. The trusty wench was now despatched on a new errand, to desire the Father to send for his relics. She understood her business, and acquainted Friar Nicolo with all that had passed. The Friar, pressed by the necessity of the affair, went to the warden of the house, and confessing the whole intrigue, begged that he would help him out in this extremity. The warden sharply reproved him for his negligence; and said there was no time to be lost, and something must be thought of to save the reputation of the Order. He therefore caused the chapter bell to be rung, and the Friars being all assembled, he informed them, that Heaven had that day wrought a most remarkable miracle, by virtue of St. Griffon's birch and breeches, in the house of Ruggieri, the physician. In short, he related to them the particulars, and persuaded them to go and fetch back the holy garment, in a solemn procession.

The Friars were now drawn up in order, and with a cross carried before them, and the warden at their head, holding the tabernacle of the altar in his hand, marched two and two in profound silence to Ruggieri's house. The doctor met them at the door, and demanded the reason of their solemn visit. The warden told him, they were obliged by the rules of their Order, to send their relics privately to such distressed persons as desired the use of them; that if through the sins of the patient, the relics had no effect, they were to fetch them as privately back; but when a manifest miracle is wrought, they were to bring them home with decent ceremony, to publish the miracle, and finally to record it in form in the register of their convent. Ruggieri now understood their business, and expressed himself overjoyed at the honour which was done him. He told the Fathers they were all welcome, and desiring the warden and Father Nicolo to follow him, he led them to his wife's chamber. The good lady, who, it may be supposed, was not asleep in this juncture, held the breeches in her hand, bound decently up in a perfumed napkin, which the warden having opened, kissed them with profound reverence; and having caused them to be kissed in like manner by all who were in the room, he put them in the tabernacle he had brought for that purpose, and gave the signal to his fraternity to return in the same order.

The Fathers set forward in greater solemnity than before, and singing an anthem, marched round the city, accompanied with a numberless crowd, and then placing the relic on the altar of their chapel, left it there, as an object of devotion. Ruggieri was zealous to promote the reverence of the people to this pious Order, and with no little ostentation, acquainted all persons, wherever he came, of the astonishing miracle wrought on his wife, by the birch and breeches of St. Griffon.

A BOY WHIPPED IN NEWGATE FOR DESTROYING WOMEN'S APPAREL WITH AQUAFORTIS.

Until severe examples were made of the actors in this kind of "frolic and fun," females often found their clothes drop to tatters, and such as restricted themselves to mere muslin and chemise were frequently dreadfully burnt, in a way invisible, and almost unaccountable. A set of urchins, neither men nor boys, by way of a "high game" procured aquafortis, vitriol, and other corrosive fluids, and filling therewith a syringe, or bottle, would sally forth to give the girls "a squirt."

Of this mischievous description we find Edward Beazley, who was convicted of this unpardonable offence at the Old Bailey, the 11th of March, 1811.

He was indicted for wilfully and maliciously injuring and destroying the apparel of Anne Parker, which she was wearing, by feloniously throwing upon the same a certain poisonous substance called aquafortis, whereby the same was so injured as to be rendered useless and of no value.

He was also charged upon two other indictments for the like offence, on the prosecution of two other women.

It appeared that the prisoner, a little boy about thirteen years old, took it into his head to sally into Fleet Street, on the night of Saturday, February 16th, and there threw the same upon the clothes of several of the Cyprians who parade up and down there. He was caught, carried before the sitting magistrate at Guildhall, and fully committed on three several charges.

Three ladies appeared, and proved the facts stated in the indictments, and exhibited their burnt garments, such as pelisses, gowns, and other articles, which were literally burnt to riddles.

He was found guilty.

His master, Mr. Blades, and an eminent chemist on Ludgate Hill, gave him a good character for honesty; he never knew anything wrong of him before; but he acknowledged that he had access to both vitriol and aquafortis.

The Court having a discretionary power under the Act of Parliament, instead of transporting him for seven years, only ordered him to be well whipped in the gaol, and returned to his friends.

ILL TREATMENT OF FEMALE PUPILS.

We frequently hear of the low-bred and licentious of our sex, ill-treating young helpless females; but to find a minister of the Gospel convicted of so base and unmanly an assault is a scandal to his functions, and an aggravated disgrace to human nature.

This abhorred man, a clergyman and schoolmaster, at Newton, near Manchester, was brought up to receive the judgment of the court of King's Bench at Westminster, in consequence of having being convicted at the last Lancaster Assizes, on two indictments, for assaulting and whipping Mary Ann Gillibrand and Mary Barlow, his scholars.

The defendant delivered in the affidavits of several females who had been his scholars in their youths, who declared upon oath, that they never saw him take the smallest liberty with his pupils in an improper way, or whip them severely, and that they thought him a fit person to he intrusted with the instruction of youth.

Mr. Scarlett addressed the Court in mitigation. The punishment, he said, the Court would feel it due to justice to inflict would be of little additional consequence to the defendant, as his ruin was alreadv consummated; but he had a wife and six children, who had been virtuously bred and educated, and it was on their account he implored the Court not to inflict a punishment on the defendant that would render him infamous.

Mr. Serjeant Cockell said it was not his wish to bruise the bended reed, yet it was necessary that an example should be made of the defendant. He was a clergyman and a teacher of youth; and the prosecutors, who had acted from the most laudable motives, had abundant reasons for what they had done. They felt themselves irresistibly called upon to check the practices imputed to the defendant, and which there was too much reason for believing he had indulged in for a considerable time past.

Mr. Justice Grose, in passing sentence, addressed the defendant to the following effect: "You have been convicted of an assault upon a child of very tender years; the narrative of your conduct is horrible to hear, and horrible to reflect upon—

the aggravations of your offence, I am sorry to say, are multifarious—the object of your brutality was a child committed to your care and instruction, and you are a teacher—a man grey in years, and possessing a large family. In looking to the class of misdemeanours, I know of none so horrible as the one of which you have been convicted. Of your guilt it is impossible to doubt, and I am shocked to see a clergyman standing to receive sentence for such an offence. Mr. Justice Grose then proceeded to pass sentence, and adjudged that the defendant should be imprisoned in Lancaster gaol for three years.

THE HON. ARTHUR WILLIAM HODGE,

ONE OF THE MEMBERS OF HIS MAJESTY'S COUNCIL IN TORTOLA, AN ISLAND SUBJECT TO GREAT BRITAIN, IN THE WEST INDIES, EXECUTED THERE ON THE 8TH OF MAY, 1811, FOR THE MURDER OF HIS NEGRO SLAVE.

> I would not have a slave to till my ground,
> To fan me when I sleep, and tremble when
> I wake, for all that human sinews bought
> And sold, have ever earn'd.
>
> COWPER.

We believe that this is the first Englishman who suffered capital punishment for flogging his own slaves to death; at least since the amelioration of their wretched condition; but we are very sure that numbers—as well French, Spaniards, Dutch, Portuguese, and above all, Americans—have deserved the fate of Hodge, for barbarity to their fellow-men, differing in nought but colour.

The greater part of Englishmen, while drinking grog, or quaffing the fumes of best Virginia; or their wives and daughters in sipping their tea, know not by what base means rum, sugar, and tobacco are imported into this country. The case before us affords an opportunity of throwing some light upon the dark subject—of bringing to public view a long continued series of barbarity—of burthens not fit for beasts to bear—of whips and chains that overpower the frailer flesh and bend the spirits down —of deliberate, cruel, wanton, and unpunished murders. Of a theme like this we may speak at large, for,

> ————————Something I'd unfold
> If that the God would wake, and something still there lies
> In Heaven's dark volume, which I read through mists;
> 'Tis black! prodigious! and now just disclosing.
> I see how terrible it dawns,
> And my soul sickens at it!
>
> DRYDEN.

The Hon. A. W. Hodge, Esq., proprietor, and one of His Majesty's Council in this Island, was indicted for the murder of one of his own negroes, of the name of Prosper.

The prisoner, on his trial, being put to the bar, pleaded Not Guilty. The first witness called to prove the charge was a free woman of colour, of the name of Pareen Georges. She stated she was in the habit of attending at Mr. Hodge's estate to wash linen; that one day Prosper came to her to borrow 6s., being the sum that his master required of him, because a mango had fallen from a tree, which he (Prosper) was set to watch. He told the witness that he must either find the 6s. or be flogged; that the witness had only 3s., which she gave him, but that it did not appease Mr. Hodge: that Prosper was flogged for upwards of an hour, receiving more than 100 lashes, and threatened by his master, that if he did not bring the remaining 3s., on the next day, the flogging should be repeated; that the next day he was tied to a tree, and flogged for such a length of time, with the thong of the whip doubled, that his head fell back, and that he could bawl no more. From thence he was carried to the sick-house, and chained to two other negroes; that he remained in this confinement during five days; at the end of which time his companions broke away, and thereby released him; that he was unable to abscond; that he went to the negro-houses and shut himself up; that he was found there dead, and in a state of putrefaction, some days afterwards; that crawlers were found in his wounds, and not a piece of black flesh was to be seen on the hinder part of his body where he had been flogged.

Stephen McKeogh, a white man, who had lived as manager on Mr. Hodge's estate, deposed, that he saw the deceased, Prosper, after he had been so severely flogged, that he could put his finger in his side; he saw him some days before his death in a cruel state; he could not get near him for the blue flies. Mr. Hodge had told the witness while he was in his employ, that if the work on the estate was not done, he was satisfied if he heard the whip.

This was the evidence against the prisoner. His counsel, in their attempt to impeach the veracity of the witnesses, called evidence as to his general character, which disclosed instances of still greater barbarity on the part of Mr. Hodge. Among other examples, the witness, Pareen Georges, swore that he had occasioned the death of his cook, named Margaret, by pouring boiling water down her throat.

Before the jury retired, the prisoner addressed them as follows:—

"Gentlemen, as bad as I have been represented, or as bad as you may think me, I assure you, that I feel support in my affliction from entertaining a proper sense of religion. As all men are subject to wrong, I cannot but say that principle is likewise inherent in me. I acknowledge myself guilty in regard to many of my slaves; but I call God to witness my innocence in respect to the murder of Prosper. I am sensible that the country thirsts for my blood, and I am ready to sacrifice it."

The jury, after deliberation, brought in a verdict of Guilty.

There were six other indictments on similar charges against the prisoner.

After, as well as previous to, his condemnation, and to the last moment of his life, Mr. Hodge persisted in his innocence of the crime for which he was about to suffer. He acknowledged that he had been a cruel master (which, as he afterwards said, was all he meant in his admission to the jury, of his guilt in regard to others of his slaves); that he had repeatedly flogged his negroes; that they had then run away, when, by their own neglect, and the consequent exposure of their wounds, the death of some of them had possibly ensued. He denied all intentions of causing the death of anyone, and pleaded the unruly and insubordinate disposition of his whole gang as the motive of his severity. These were the sentiments in which he died.

Governor Elliot sent to Lord Liverpool the depositions of the witnesses who were examined on this trial. The deposition of Mr. Robertson stated that he had every reason to suspect Mr. Hodge of having murdered five of his slaves!

The Governor then mentioned the proceedings he had thought proper to adopt; giving an account of the trial and conviction of Mr. Hodge—the majority of the petit jury recommended him to mercy! but none of the judges seconded the recommendation.

From the period of his condemnation to his execution, Governor Elliot thought it expedient to proclaim martial law, and to embody the militia; but no disturbance took place. However, the Governor added, that "the state of irritation, nay, I had almost said, of anarchy, in which I have found this colony, rendered the above measures indispensable for the preservation of tranquility, and for ensuring the due execution of the sentence against Arthur W. Hodge. Indeed, it is but too probable that without my presence, in a conjunction so replete with party animosity, unpleasant occurrences might have ensued."

SECT OF FLAGELLANTS.

A general plague, which swept away a vast multitude of people, gave rise to the fanatic sect of flagellants or whippers, whom this scourge had awakened to a sense of religion.

Henault.

They established themselves at Perouse, A.D. 1260. They maintained that there was no remission of sins without flagellation, and publicly lashed themselves, while in procession preceded by the cross, until the blood flowed from their naked backs. Their leader, Conrad Schmidt, was burnt 1414.

FLOGGING WITH A FRYING-PAN.

At the Woolwich Police-court, December 29th, 1882, an elderly man, named James Bone, was charged on a summons before Mr. Mersham with assaulting Margaret Chapmann.

The complainant, a widow, said that the defendant engaged her to go to his house in Nun Street, Woolwich, and do a day's washing. There was no other person in the house, and the defendant told her he had turned his wife out of doors. About midday he gave her a glass of spirits, which took such effect that she did not remember whether she had any more or not. She remembered no more until the evening, when she found herself lying undressed upon the floor, and the defendant pouring water over her from a pail. He had stripped her of everything, and beaten her with some weapon about the body until she was covered with bruises from head to foot. As soon as she recovered sufficiently she ran out of the house to escape from his violence, and some women got clothing for her.

Defendant said he gave the woman a glass of stout with her luncheon, and afterwards a glass of brandy. He went out in the afternoon, and when he returned, he found that she had drunk a pint of rum, and was in a shocking state of intoxication. She stripped herself, and tried to go to bed, but fell helpless on the floor, and he then bathed her with some cold water, spoiling his new carpet, and also tried to bring her to her senses by flogging her with the hot frying-pan. (Laughter.) He did not deny causing her bruises, for he hit her perhaps a hundred times, and if she had not been so heavy he would have thrown her out of the window. He tied a rope round her feet, but could not drag her out of the room, and, after giving her some more water, she got up and walked into the street just as she was. He was so disgusted that if he could have got a gun he would have shot her. All that he could do was to send for a cab and get her away.

Mrs. Catherine Limey said that she had occasion to go to the house on business, and the defendant showed her the complainant lying stripped upon the carpet. She got up on hearing a woman's voice and ran into the street. There were several weals upon her body, and her clothes had evidently been torn from her with violence.

Mr. Mersham remanded the defendant in custody for a week.

MEMORY BY WHIPPING.

A "striking" instance of mnemonics is communicated to *Notes and Queries* by one of its correspondents :—Gilles de Retz, Marshal of France (said to be the veritable Blue Beard) was sentenced to be led in chains to the place of execution, and to be burnt alive at the stake. The day appointed was October 23, 1440, "a date," says the historian, "about which there can be no doubt, for all the people of Anjou and Maine, by common consent, whipped their children on that morning, *so as to impress the precise date on their memory.*" This strange mnemonic process is still a favourite with the peasants of Anjou and Brittany.

EXTRACT FROM THE REVELATIONS OF BIRCHINGTON GRANGE.

Asking for a good birch-rod, the Colonel says he will show them the way a real expert would use it, whisking the birch about so that the trembling victim can hear it hissing through the air.

The Colonel continues," Now the real art of birching consists, of course, in inflicting the greatest amount of humiliation and suffering, but without in reality doing serious damage ; we have to consider how so to apply the rod as to effect some radical moral good in the disposition and mind of the guilty culprit ; how to make them feel the very dregs, as it were, of humiliation, degradation, and every kind of mortification. It is a curious fact that it sends the blood of a sensitive modest girl in impulsive rushes (especially to the face and neck) in the shape of scarlet or crimson blushes, which pass over those parts in continuous waves, corresponding to each stroke of the rod ; this is a curious psychological fact, which is puzzling even to anatomists.

"Ah! I begin to see what kind of a young lady you really are, and I am very much impressed with the idea that you are radically naughty and obstinate; it's very painful to me, every stroke sends the blood rushing through my veins; it's a kind of weakness or sympathy for your suffering, but I must not let it prevent me from doing my duty."

LETTER FROM MRS. MASTINET ON SLIPPER PUNISHMENT.

A slipper is a splendid thing to whip or slap with, as it has such a stinging effect without cutting the skin, like a regular birch-rod.

I should not write so fully as I do, but knowing you to be an amateur flagellant, and consequently, interested in every incident of punishment, it gives a kind of freedom to my pen, as I know you can be depended on not to abuse my confidence.

My special penchant used to be for the use of a good stinging bunch of real birch twigs, and I still think that is far the best thing to use for big girls over thirteen, but for little delicate chits under that age, there is nothing answers so well as a nice new slipper; a proficient disciplinarian would first give the delinquent a short lecture on the nature of her offence, then firmly insist upon the culprit herself fetching the instrument of punishment: to my idea, there is more shame and humiliation at having to bring the slipper to be whipped, than fear of the smart, which is always worse in imagination than fact.

A skilful flagellatrix will always prolong these sensations, as they effect as much good as the application of the slipper.

A HUNGARIAN SCANDAL.

[FROM OUR CORRESPONDENT AT VIENNA.]

The scandal reported from Hungary is prominently discussed by the Vienna press. The facts of the case are these. During the Autumn Manœuvres in the neighbourhood of Miscolcz, a number of cavalry soldiers were billeted at the house of a respectable country gentleman named Nicolas Bizony. The latter, an elderly man, happened to have a trifling dispute with the troopers, which was overheard by the inspecting officer. Without making a proper inquiry the officer ordered the old man to be corporally chastised in a particularly humiliating fashion. Bizony lodged a complaint with the district commander, and after the matter had been discussed by a council of officers, a formal apology was made. The officer who had ordered the assault begged the old man on his knees to forgive him, which Bizony readily consented to do, and further promised to say nothing more about it to anyone. But a short time ago it came to the ears of the local magistrate, and was afterwards reported to the Imperial Chancellerie. Bizony refused to furnish information, but eyewitnesses of what had happened were not so discreet. Apprehending a judicial inquiry, and being unwilling to break his word, Bizony shot himself through the heart, and thus died a victim of his own generosity. The officer by whose commands Bizony was beaten appears to have put forward the excuse that he thought he was a Jew. Bizony had a son in the army, and was himself universally esteemed. The matter will most likely be taken in hand by the Emperor, and the guilty party dealt with as he deserves.

FLOGGING AND CRUELTY IN A GLASGOW INDUSTRIAL SCHOOL.

A case not unlike what has just been been brought to light in London is reported in connection with the Glasgow Girls' Industrial School. The charges against the matron, consist of acts of cruelty when administering punishment to the girls. Here is part of an account given in a Glasgow paper of an interview with the matron regarding her treatment of a girl, who had absconded from the institution. The girl was taken into the laundry with only her chemise and a petticoat on, and held by two girls while she (the matron) flogged her with the "tawse." She knows that the girl's garments got twisted in the struggle, but cannot remember whether they all came off or not. Is sure that the girl did not receive more than twelve strokes, very likely not so many. After flogging the girl she went to her own room, she was so excited, leaving instructions to have the girl put under the spray-bath to cool her down. After whipping the girls she gave them the spray-bath to revive them. Then a mattress was taken into the surgery and the girl was put in there. That very night she visited her in the surgery, and told her she had only punished her for her good. She taught her a little prayer, and then prayed with her. The account of the interview goes on to say, "You did not enter the punishment in the punishment book?—No. Why?—Because the girl had never been in the school-room, and the punishment did not form part of the ordinary discipline of the school. You consider that the punishment requisite to break a girl in should not be entered?—Well, I go upon precedent. I was assistant to the former matron, and in a case where a girl was punished under similar circumstances it was not entered in the book. It does not belong to the regular discipline of the school."

The matron mentioned above is also reported by the same girl to have confessed to stripping a girl naked before whipping her. This lady, who was assistant matron, said she knew nothing about the rules. One of the teachers who has since left the institution said she did so out of disgust at the way it was conducted, and the cruelty practised in the punishment of the inmates. The resignation of the matron had been accepted by the committee of directors appointed to inquire into the case.

CRUELTY TO A PUPIL.

The head master of Colfe's Grammar School was summoned for assaulting a pupil in his school.

The complainant, a lad of 13, said that he had been in the school for four years, and was in the class of one of the assistant masters. On the 14th of November he was told to "stand out," as a punishment for talking. He did so, and by accident trod upon a nutshell. He was then told he should "stand out" for two days. Next day he was told to write pages, the number mentioned being four. He wrote some of them in the morning, and then went home to dinner. He returned in the afternoon, and the assistant master then gave him a letter to take to the defendant. (A solicitor read the letter, which stated that he could do nothing with Johnson, and asked the head master to punish him; but not to make the punishment too light.) Complainant said that he did not deliver the letter, but he took it home with him. Next morning a note was received from the head master stating that he could not receive witness back, in consequence of his misconduct. His sister went and apologised, and he was told to return next morning, which he did. The defendant took him into the library, and told him to take down his trousers. He did so, and the defendant then lifted up his shirt, laid him across his knee, and gave him four cuts across the lower part of the body with a cane. In cross-examination, the complainant admitted that he had been caned before, three or four times; but never in this manner. He had been reported for misconduct, and had been "isolated," that is, set apart from the boys.

A nurse deposed to having examined the boy. There were wales on the body.

The solicitor alluded to the satisfactory reports made of the complainant at the school, and submitted that the punishment had been unduly severe. He was a bright and high-spirited boy. The punishment did not incapacitate the boy; but it seemed to him to have been inflicted with brutal severity.

Defendant's solicitor then addressed the Court for the defence, and stated that the boy had shown signs of disaffection; and, according to his own evidence, had been punished repeatedly for misconduct.

The Magistrate said he could not say that the punishment was excessive, although severe. He thought that, perhaps, a birch-rod would be a more suitable instrument of punishment, and was of opinion that a head master should be at liberty to punish boys. He dismissed the summons, remarking that persons should consider well before proceeding against a schoolmaster, as such proceedings affected his character.

The parties then left the Court.

G. A. S. ON THE ROD.

Solomon said, in accents mild,
Spare the rod and spoil the child;
Be they man or be they maid,
Whip and wallop 'em, Solomon said.

The dicta of the Wise Man concerning discipline have been the source of inexpressible dolour to children for very many centuries; and it has only been within the last sixty years that ferocity in the treatment of infants (I am speaking of English children, Jean Jacques Rousseau shamed the French out of the practice of beating their offspring, nearly a hundred years ago) has been gradually diminishing. In the eighteenth century the lot of the British juvenile was certainly a cruel one. That admirable woman, the mother of the Wesleys, held that a child should be made to desist from crying and to "fear the rod" at the mature age of twelve months; and Miss Maria Semple, writing on education, in 1812, tells a story of a lady who was educated in early years by a relative. "On a certain day in every week she received corporal chastisement. If she had committed faults, 'the punishment was due;' if she had not, she probably would in the week ensuing. At the distance of more than half-a-century, the memory of this person, who bore a public character of piety and virtue, was spoken of, and justly, with aversion by the person she had thus treated." Thus Miss Maria Semple.—" G. A. S." in the *Illustrated London News.*

THE CONVENT SCHOOL.

The Superior, with whom Olive had been a favourite, now vented her spite in every direction amongst the young lady pupils of the seminary, and I, for one, soon fell under her displeasure, and was ordered to be tied up to the whipping-post. It was only for slightly oversleeping myself, and not dressing quickly, when the bell rang for us to get up at 6 a.m. I was suspended by my wrists, being tied high up the post, as I stood upon a small footstool, when it was suddenly kicked away, the jerk of the sudden strain on my wrists almost making the straps cut into the flesh. My feet were dangling some inches from the ground. "Oh! oh! Ah-r-r-r-re!" I screamed. "How cruel! Oh! Papa! Papa! if you only knew how they are treated in this awful place."

The Lady Superior (who seemed delighted at the sight of my pain)—"Hold your foolish noise, Mdlle. Lucille; wait till you have something to scream about, girl." Then the old Serena, who it seemed was always in attendance at punishment time, pinned up my skirts, and the Superior went on, "This rod shall make all the sluggards turn out quicker in the morning. What do you think, Mademoiselle, of making us all wait prayers for ten minutes? Will you wake—wake up sharper in future?"

She then gave me several severe cuts with the rod. My screams were heartrending, but they only seemed to enjoy it more and more, and the Superior never ended her objurgations till the rod was worn out.

MORE LETTERS ON CORPORAL PUNISHMENT.

"E. S." (A Music Master) writes: "I have read the correspondence relating to the personal chastisement of young ladies in your pages with great interest; and as your correspondent who signs himself "Rector" seems to doubt its application, I just write a few lines from my own personal observation to convince him to the contrary. I am a teacher of music in five schools conducted by ladies, and in two of these the most strict discipline is kept up. When I am giving a music lesson the lady principal remains in the room, and the pupils keep continually coming one at a time to have their ciphering and writing books, &c., inspected; and if these are untidily kept, or the pupil has not been diligent, she is ordered to hold out her hand, and receives several smart slaps on the palm with an instrument which I will proceed to describe. It consists of a leathern strap, narrowed at one end to fit the hand of the schoolmistress, and divided at the other end into five tails. The consequence is that each strip of leather inflicts a separate blow upon the pupil's hand; and the punishment, although sufficiently severe, leaves no bruise upon the hand; in this respect, having a great advantage over the cane. With this strap there is no danger of seriously injuring the hand; and the pain, although severe, soon passes off, and leaves no permanent effects; and it has this advantage over the birch, that there is no exposure, and the age of the pupil is of no consequence. This, I think is of great importance, as my experience has convinced me that it is not always the youngest pupils in a school who require correction. I have frequently seen this punishment applied to the hands of pupils of sixteen years of age, and I am quite sure that it is productive of the most beneficial effects. I am certain most of your readers will agree with me, that the use of the birch is quite out of the question with young ladies of this age; and the most convincing proof of the utility of this kind of punishment lies in the fact that in both of these schools where corporal punishment is inflicted the lessons are invariably gone through better than in any of the other three where it is not used, and the behaviour of the pupils is much more ladylike. To my mind this mode of punishment is by far the best, and it is easily applied. The age of the pupil is not of much importance, and the palm of a young lady's hand is sufficiently sensitive to allow of a tolerably severe punishment being inflicted; and my opinion is that punishment should be seldom inflicted, but when it is required it should be sharp and severe. It is very seldom indeed that I am compelled to report a pupil to the lady principal, but whenever I am compelled to do so punishment is promptly inflicted, and the pupil is always more attentive the next lesson. In conclusion, I must say that I cannot understand why this kind of punishment on the hand, to which boys are so freely subjected, should be considered inapplicable to young ladies."

"Medical Student" writes: "With regard to the Whipping of Girls, I think that, as 'this is the age of the ladies,' there is no reason why girls should not be whipped as well as boys. But let me remind some of your correspondents that the days in which Milton was whipped at Oxford are long gone by, and if the girls require to be whipped at sixteen they will require it all their lives. I suppose that their husbands are the only persons on whom the duty will devolve after they have left the parental mansion. Now, as husbands are punished for thrashing their wives, why should not schoolmistresses be punished for doing the same by young ladies of sixteen or seventeen committed to their care?"

"Gratitude." "I own, as you see, one of the most honoured names in England, and call myself 'Gratitude,' because I am anxious to show my gratitude for the fact that I owe my present position as a useful, happy English lady to the firm discipline I experienced at the very turning-point of my life. I was brought up in a loving home, I had every possible

A.Z.

advantage; but amidst it all I became sullen, self-willed, and disobedient and idle. I was the grief of my parents and a byword to my companions. However, soon after I was fifteen I most fortunately was sent to Mrs. ——'s school for young ladies, in Brighton, where I showed the same evil disposition which I had evinced elsewhere, but where, most fortunately and happily for me, it was checked and cured. In school and out of it, during the first month, Mrs. —— and the other teachers reproved me, set me tasks, and 'kept me in.' But I only grew worse; and one night, after I had refused to do an 'imposition,' as boys call a punishment lesson, Mrs. —— came and sat in my room after I was in bed, and talked to me most impressively. The next day, however, the impression of what she had said wore off, and I was as bad as ever. But a change was at hand, for in the evening, when we had just gone to our bedrooms, Mrs. —— again came to me, and said, 'Miss W., you will to-night occupy the dressing-room adjoining my room. I will show the way.' I was half inclined to disobey. However, I followed my governess through her bedroom and across a small sitting-room, which opened out of it into a room comfortably furnished, in which was a small low bed, and telling me to undress and go to bed, Mrs. —— left me, locking the door after her. I had been in bed about a quarter of an hour when Mrs. —— came to me, holding in her hand a long birch-rod. Placing the candlestick and the rod on the table, she told me that but one course was now open to her after my behaviour, and that she was going to flog me, and I was to get up. But though the twigs of the birch-rod stood out in ominous shadow in front of the candlestick, and while I noted the thin, closely-wrapped handle of that rod, and its fanlike-spreading top, I never attempted to obey. Three t mes Mrs. —— told me to get up, but I stirred not. She then very deliberately turned down the bedclothes, and again told me to get out of bed. I began to feel that I was going to be conquered, but yet I stirred not. Mrs. —— returned to her own room, and came back with a small, thin riding-whip, and said, 'Must I use this?' There was something about her which quite awed me—it was more her manner than her tall, powerful figure—and as she swung the whip about in her hand I at once stepped out of bed and stood before her. 'Give me your hands,' she said, but I put them behind me, when slash across my shoulders came six or seven smart strokes of her whip, and screaming I put out my hands, which she fastened together with a cord by the wrists. Then making me lie down across the foot of the bed, face downwards, she very quietly and deliberately, putting her left hand round my waist, gave me a shower of smart slaps with her open right hand—a proceeding which so surprised and humiliated my proud self that I could hardly believe in my own identity, and as I screamed and struggled, she merely said, 'This is for not doing *now* as I told you, and it will not only punish you for *that*, but will increase the pain of the birching I am now going to give you.' Mrs. —— then, as I lay, spoke to me for a few minutes with great kindness and earnestness. She then rose, took the birch in her right hand, and stooping over me, pressed her left hand tightly on my shoulder so as to hold me as if I were in a vice; then raising the birch, I could hear it whiz in the air, and oh, how terrible it felt as it came down, and as its repeated strokes came swish, swish, swish, on me! yet I felt, spite of the terrible stinging pain, that I deserved it all—and it *was* painful. I was a stout, fair girl, and very sensitive to pain. I screamed, I protested, I implored, but it was of no avail; Mrs. —— heeded not my cries, but held me down and birched on till she had finished a whipping which seemed to last an age, but which quite changed my character. At last it *was* over. I was permitted to rise, my hands were unbound, and, burning and smarting, I raised my tear-stained face to my true friend's, on whose face no sign was visible, of the slightest anger or passion. Calm and serene, she wished me 'Good-night,' and left me conquered. Henceforward I was a different girl; and though a few weeks afterwards I relapsed, yet another night spent in Mrs. ——'s dressing-room, and another similar application by her of that wonder-working birch—I did exactly as she told me this time—sufficed finally to cure me. I became cheerful, obedient, unselfish. My parents and friends the next holidays could hardly believe that I was the same girl. I stayed three years with Mrs. —— at Brighton, leaving her when I was nineteen with much regret. I am now twenty-four, and hope to be married at Easter to *the best man in the world*, who never *could* have loved me had not sensible, wholesome discipline changed my evil nature, as *the* means under Higher Power of doing so. I am thankful to publish my experience, and so to express not only my gratitude, but confirm what others have so well said and told on this subject."

"Emma" (near Newcastle) writes: "A while ago I undertook to bring up two nieces, of the ages of twelve and fourteen. I soon found them to be most stubborn tempers and impudent. Thus they have often caused me much trouble and annoyance. Though not an advocate of corporal punishment, I was much struck with the description by 'A Schoolmistress' of a most ceremonious method of inflicting punishment that I determined to follow exactly the same method and try it the same morning. I prepared a woollen dress; not being able to procure a birch, I sent and had made a pair of very long pliant leather taws. In the afternoon I found the eldest of my nieces in a gross fault, and on being found fault with she was very pert. I therefore took her to my bedroom and made her don the garment and follow me to the drawing-room, she never thinking for a moment of what was to follow. I then quietly told her of her bad conduct for some time past, and that I was determined to try what a whipping would do. On ordering her to lay across an ottoman she distinctly refused. I told her if she did not at once comply I would ring for a servant to compel her. Still refusing, I rang for assistance. Hearing the servant coming upstairs, and seeing me determined, she lay down, rather than be seen by the servant in this predicament, wherefore I went to the door and sent the servant back. I then fastened her across the ottoman. I then proceeded to administer a few strokes of the taws, which soon elicited cries for forgiveness and promises of future good conduct, but being determined to try the efficacy of this method, I continued until I had given her a severe flogging. I then allowed her to rise, and on her knees to thank me for the correction, then sent her off to bed for the day. Up to this time the perfect subjection and submission of this girl is such that I most heartily recommend all parents and guardians to try the same method in all cases of disobedience. I think that in all whippings of grown children a large amount of cool ceremony is most effectual."

"An Old Boy" writes: "Since the question of the efficacy of Corporal Punishment seems to give rise to a great variety of opinions, I venture to give mine. When a boy I was educated at Christ's Hospital, and I assure you the birch was not neglected there, and generally with beneficial effects. The punishment was sometimes inflicted privately, but when the offence was serious, due publicity was given it. The offender after supper was made to stand opposite the Warden's desk, and hold the instrument of torture in his hand (it being customary for punishments to be doled out after that meal). When the boys had retired (with the exception of the ward to which the delinquent belonged, who were ordered to remain in their seats), two of the school porters were summoned, and the offender was told to prepare himself. He was then hoisted on the back of one of the porters, when the other with great deliberation proceeded to remove all unnecessary clothing by tucking the inner garment beneath the back of his coat, and after having measured his distance, commenced the punishment, always allowing a little time between each stroke, so as to give them due effect. The offender having received the allotted number was let down, and after finishing his toilet was allowed to retire with his schoolfellows, who generally condoled with him if he bore it well. After once receiving a punishment of this kind it seldom required to be repeated. But it would be a good thing if schoolmasters, guardians, and parents, would study the characters of the children committed to their charge, as they would soon ascertain what punishments would be most effectual. I am convinced that flogging does not suit every case, though it might be effectual in extreme ones; but I think it is a great mistake to suppose that that is the only punishment that ought to be inflicted, as in some cases a word would be more effectual, especially with sensitive children. I am surprised that girls should require such correction, but I am acquainted with one or two to whom a good wholesome flogging would indeed be a great boon both to themselves and their parents."

ELIZABETH BROWNRIGG,

EXECUTED AT TYBURN, SEPTEMBER 14, 1767, FOR TORTURING HER FEMALE APPRENTICES TO DEATH.

The long scene of torture in which this inhuman woman kept the innocent object of her remorseless cruelty, ere she finished the long-premeditated murder, engaged the interest of the superior ranks, and roused the indignation of the populace, more than any criminal in the whole course of our experience.

This cruel woman having passed the early part of her life in the service of private families, was married to James Brownrigg, a plumber, who, after being seven years in Greenwich, came to London, and took a house in Flower-de-luce Court, Fleet Street, where he carried on a considerable share of business, and had a little house at Islington, for an occasional retreat.

She had been the mother of sixteen children, and having practised midwifery, was appointed by the overseers of the poor of St. Dunstan's parish, to take care of the poor women who were taken in labour in the workhouse; which duty she performed to the entire satisfaction of her employers.

Mary Mitchell, a poor girl, of the precinct of Whitefriars, was put apprentice to Mrs. Brownrigg in the year 1765; and about the same time Mary Jones, one of the children of the Foundling Hospital, was likewise placed with her in the same capacity; and she had other apprentices.

As Mrs. Brownrigg received women to lie-in privately, these girls were taken with a view of saving the expense of women servants. At first the poor orphans were treated with some degree of civility; but this was soon changed for the most savage barbarity.

Having laid Mary Jones across two chairs in the kitchen, she whipped her with such wanton cruelty, that she was occasionally obliged to desist through mere weariness.

This treatment was frequently repeated; and Mrs. Brownrigg used to throw water on her when she had done whipping her.

On one occasion she caused the girl to strip to the skin, and during the course of a whole day, while she remained naked, she repeatedly beat her with the butt end of a whip.

In the course of this most inhuman treatment, a jack-chain was fastened round her neck, the end of which was fastened to the yard door, and then it was pulled as tight as possible, without strangling her.

A day being passed in the practice of these savage barbarities, the girl was remanded to the coal-hole at night, l er hands being tied behind her, and the chain still remaining about her neck.

The husband having been obliged to find his wife's apprentices in wearing-apparel, they were repeatedly stript naked, and kept so for whole days, if their garments happened to be torn.

At the ensuing sessions at the Old Bailey, Elizabeth Brownrigg, after a trial of eleven hours, was found Guilty of murder, and after a sentence of death was passed, she was attended by a clergyman, to whom she confessed the enormity of her crime, and acknowledged the justice of the sentence.

MARY KNIGHT,

EXECUTED AT WARWICK, AUGUST 24, 1778, FOR THE MURDER OF HER CHILD.

Though we have gone through the painful task of relating instances of women murdering their offspring, yet the commission of such unnatural barbarity has generally happened with such unfortunate females as have been seduced and betrayed, and in that wretched situation, vainly hoping to conceal their shame, they have killed the innocent pledge of their illicit love.

But the case of Mary Knight, seems to contain no cause to be assigned for the foul crime; on the contrary, nothing short of wanton brutality seems to have led her on to this most shocking sin; and to complete the horror of the tale, she was convicted chiefly on the evidence of her younger son, a child not nine years of age.

The story of the child was credible. He said that his mother sent his brother into the stubble-fields to glean, that when he came home, his mother beat him in a most cruel manner with a great stick, for not bringing more corn; that he cried sadly, and she shut him up in the pantry; that some time after the witness called to him to come and play, but he made no answer; that he opened the pantry-door, took hold of his hand, and it felt cold.

Then the child further said, that he went to his mother, and told her that Roger (the deceased) felt cold, and begged her to let him come to the fire. His mother then went into the pantry, and brought Roger, wrapped up in her apron, and carried him out of doors; she shut the door after her, but he looked under it, and saw her throw him into the well; that when she came in again, she put the stick she had beaten him with into the fire; that before it was entirely consumed, the neighbours came in, who immediately took the deceased out of the well, and the stick out of the fire.

The latter part of the child's evidence respecting the dead body and the stick with which his brother had been beaten, was corroborated by the neighbours, and the burnt stick was produced in court. On this evidence she was convicted and executed.

THE WOMAN IN WHITE.

Mme. Hautville made a very pretty toilette for the occasion —she was all in white; in the costume of a novice when she takes the veil. The dress had been considerably modified, as being too flowing for the occasion, but it was all white silk and lace; and a lovely little angel she looked when it was complete From head to foot she had nothing on that was not pure white. White satin shoes, with diamonds sparkling on the rosettes; white silk stockings, gartered above her round knees with white velvet garters, with satin rosettes; white petticoats—one of the finest flannel—embroidered with lilies, and one of soft lawn, with a lace flounce. Her robe was silk—the soft noiseless sort that does not rustle—richly trimmed with costly Mechlin lace; and over her head she had a square veil. She had her maid in to assist at her toilette, and fasten her garters and shoes. Madame submitted to be blindfolded with a very good grace, though she tried hard to get us to tell her what was going to be done; she had such pretty coaxing ways that it was hard to resist her; but we did, and she went in quite unprepared.

We led her slowly up the room, and at the first stroke of the rod, nearest the door, she winced, but did not cry out; the next blow she received was a stinging one from a slipper my lady held in her hand (she knows how to strike with a shoe, I can tell you), and she gave a little scream and a jump. "Oh! what is it?" she said between her teeth; but the next stroke, a fair open-handed slap from Mrs. D——'s fat hand, made her fairly shriek out, and twist herself out of her grasp on to the floor. It *was* a slap, and rang out even above the laughter of the ladies, leaving a broad red mark on the white, firm flesh of the little lady.

RUTH IN THE SCHOOLROOM.

Casting an appealing look thither, Ruth rushes into the ranks of the condemned, who all fall from around her, or become her active enemies; conspicuous among the latter are the whipped ones; they slip off their garters, jump upon a form, and adroitly catching up the struggler's wrists, secure them together by a double knot. The trained tormentors then dash in, and in half a crack reduce her to the semblance of an Albanian chief.

> In crimson tunic, light and snowy kilt,
> Lacking but yatagan and poniard hilt

The strongest twirling round their hand the aforesaid kilt, employ it as a lever to support the back-thrown bust, and pull her prancing on.

Vain all her writhings and contortions odd,
  The licking lady with sardonic grin
Withholds—but only for a space—the rod,
  Watching the happy moment to whip *in.*
As whip she will, or soon or late of course,
  Seeing the deadly purpose in her eye,
Her victim turns the reluctant thigh,
  When down it comes with desolating force,
And worn to fragments, is again renewed.
  Tho' half a glance the punishment had told
Before the kicking devil was subdued,
  That Ruth, for such correction, was too old.

Romance of Chastisement.

A SPOILT CHILD.

"A Spoilt Child" writes: "My parents were always opposed to whipping, and I was sent to a school where no corporal punishment was permitted. The natural result was, I grew up indolent, sullen, and disobedient. But, although I am now eighteen years of age, I would willingly submit myself to be flogged for my many faults each time one was committed, if such could be done. I quite agree that if an institution existed where sinful young people were subjected to whipping for their sins, it would be productive of much good. In fact, so great is my confidence in the efficacy of the rod, that if anyone would condescend to permit me to call upon them and confess my sins to them, leaving them to mete out the punishment to me, and advise me of the best manner to rid myself of my faults, I believe they would save me from ultimate ruin, and they themselves would have the satisfaction of knowing they had put me in the right road, and I should have reason to bless them as long as I live.

MISS BIRCHED FOR THIEVING.

"G. A. N." writes: "A neighbour of mine told me a few nights ago the mode she adopted for curing her daughter, aged sixteen, of the baneful habit of pilfering. She had discovered the girl in the very act of taking money from a drawer in the bedroom, and this being the third time the girl had been detected (the first and second being passed over with a mere reprimand), she determined to give her a good whipping, and having purchased a rod for the purpose, told the delinquent to go to her bedroom and prepare by taking off her drawers. In a few minutes she went upstairs, and having fastened the girl across the bed, birched her severely. The fruit of the punishment was, that from that time the girl gradually improved, and is now finally cured.

"Miss C." had several young apprentices, on some of whom she inflicted the punishment of the rod. She was not very sorry when they gave her an opportunity of handling this instrument of pleasure and pain. Among her apprentices was a slip of a girl, addicted to thieving, and though she had whipped her very often for it with severity, the girl did not amend in the least. One day as she was going to whip her for stealing some ribbons, one of the working women, who had been in Paris for many years, told her, if she was to dip the rod in vinegar, as she had seen it done in France, it would smart her the more. Miss C. followed her advice, dipped the end of a new birch-rod in a vessel full of vinegar, and whipped the girl with it with the utmost exertion of her arm; and it smarted so sore that she never pilfered after.

LADY PREPARING FOR BIRCHING.

"The beautiful colour and proportion of your arm is inimitable, and your hand is dazzling, fine, small and plump! long pointed fingers, delicately turned; dimpled on the snowy outside, but adorned within with roses, all over the soft palm. O Iris! nothing equals your fair hand, that hand, of which Love so often makes such use to draw his bow, when he would send the arrow home with more success; and which irresistibly wounds those, who possibly have not yet seen your eyes: and when you have been veiled, that lovely hand had gained you a thousand adorers! and I heard Damon say, that without the aid of more beauties, that alone had been sufficient to have made an absolute conquest over his soul. And he has often vowed it never touched him but it made his blood run with little irregular motions in his veins, his breath beat short and double, his blushes rise, and his very soul dance!"

Mrs. Behn's Novels.

"There! my dear, there's a charming description for you! What magic in every sentence! What genius could soar beyond it! Is there a heart existing but would bound with rapture on seeing such a hand exercise a rod?"

"Bless me," said Clarissa, "you talk as if you were as fond of the sport as the most enthusiastic of them."

"I confess it freely," said Flirtilla, "I am fond of it to excess, when the object inflames my blood and administers it with irresistible grace!"

"Grace! grace!" said Clarissa. "I protest I cannot comprehend your meaning."

"Know then, thou silly girl, there is a manner in handling this sceptre of felicity that few ladies are happy in: it is not the impassioned and awkward brandish of a vulgar female that can charm, but the deliberate and elegant manner of a woman of rank and fashion, who displays all that dignity in every action, even to the flirting of her fan, that leaves an indelible wound. What a difference between high and low life in this particular! To see a vulgar woman when provoked by her children, seize them as a tiger would a lamb, and correct them with an open hand, or a rod more like a broom than a neat collection of twigs elegantly tied together; while a well-bred lady, coolly and deliberately brings her child or pupil to task, and when in error, so as to deserve punishment, commands the incorrigible Miss to bring her the rod, go on her knees, and beg with uplifted hands an excellent whipping; which is administered with the loveliest hands imaginable."

HOME SCENES.

Mrs. Eden was brought up in a convent. Her parents were Roman Catholics, and having no daughter but her, they were desirous of bestowing upon her every accomplishment, and foolishly imagined a convent education far superior to any this country could boast of. There she lived till she had gained her five-and-twentieth year, at which time her father died, and she found herself in possession of twenty-five thousand pounds. At the importunities of a fond mother, who went to see her once every year, she visited England, and being a girl of good fortune it is not to be wondered at that she had a crowd of admirers. In her visits, she was very much taken with that part of a widower's family, that in general is found most disagreeable, at least to young ladies—I mean his children. She observed they were indulged by a weak father in everything, and were consequently very disobedient and unruly. Upon this gentleman, though verging upon forty, she fixed her affections, and being a woman of ungovernable spirit, she was happy to find him an easy pusillanimous creature. The match was scarcely mentioned when it was concluded, and in a few days after, she found herself in the seat of empire in his house. She had six little subjects to govern, three of whom were then at school in Herefordshire, who were instantly ordered home, as she said she would undertake to finish their education, which indeed was in her power, for she was a very sensible woman; but that was not her intent altogether. It was the boys that were ordered from school, who seemed very happy in leaving a place so irksome to youth in general; but they had only exchanged a male for a female flagellator. As soon as she was married she discharged all the servants, and hired a set of her own choosing, and among the rest she took care to engage a French lady as her own woman, whose disposition she knew would just suit her.

Mrs. Eden was of the first order of beauty, had a noble person, fine-turned limbs, good skin, fine blue eyes, as brilliant as Venus', and when not ruffled by passion, was certainly very captivating. If she had stepped across the room she discovered uncommon dignity and elegance, and every motion expressed that *Je ne scai quoi* an elegant French woman is so idolised for. In short, my dear, I never think of her without exclaiming with the poet,

> O with what bloom, what flower of youth she shone;
> How her cheeks blush'd a colour all her own,
> A genuine red, like roses newly blown!
> With her what woman could pretend to vie
> A whiter forehead, or a lovelier eye?
> Whose frame was like the world, an eloquent soul
> Spoke in each part, and sparkl'd thro' the whole;
> Each limb did wanton Loves and Graces bear;
> There lodg'd their arms, their bows and arrows there!

Though this whipping passion was inextinguishable within her, yet she was never observed to take the rod in hand without some offence to occasion it. She was convinced where there was such a number of children, and they ungovernable, many bickerings would arise, which would give her an opportunity to amuse herself with the rod. The first that gave her occasion to handle the rod was a boy of seventeen years old, who was so stupid at a lesson she gave him, that she was resolved to try the effects of birching. Her French woman was ordered to bring an excellent rod, which she had no sooner done, than she proceeded to exercise it; but she found the boy too strong for her. The maid, with the assistance of her mistress, ties his hands behind him, and then they found him manageable enough, and the woman holding his legs, his step-mother whipped him till the twigs flew about the room.

This was the first sample of her severity with the rod she gave since she was married, and it made such an impression on the rest of the children that they trembled in her presence. A few hours after the boy was complaining, with tears, of her treatment, to his elder sister, who advised him to burn the rod the first opportunity. This was overheard by the maid, who informed her lady of the affair. The young lady was summoned to the parlour, where she denied the fact, was confronted by the maid, and well whipped.

MONKS AND THEIR CONVENTS.

By Maria Monk.

But I must now come to one deed in which I had some part, and which I look back upon with greater horror and pain than any occurrence in the Convent, in which I was not the principal sufferer. It is not necessary for me to attempt to excuse myself in this or any other case. Those who have any disposition to judge fairly will excuse their own judgment in making allowances for me, under the fear and force, the command and examples before me. I, therefore, shall confine myself, as usual, to the simple narration of facts. The time was about five months after I took the veil; the weather was cool, perhaps in September or October; one day the Superior sent for me and several other nuns to receive her commands at a particular room. We found the bishops and some priests with her, and speaking in an unusual tone of fierceness and authority, she said, "Go to the room for the examination of conscience, and drag St. Frances upstairs." Nothing was more necessary than this unusual command, with the tone and manner which accompanied it, to excite in me most gloomy anticipations. It did not strike me as strange that St. Frances should be in the room to which the Superior directed us. It was an apartment to which we were often sent to prepare for the communion, and to which we voluntarily went, whenever we felt the compunctions which our ignorance of duty, and the misinstructions we received, inclined us to seek relief from self-reproach. Indeed, I had seen her there a little before. What terrified me was, first, the Superior's angry manner; second, the expression she used, being a French term, whose peculiar use I had learnt in the Convent, and whose meaning is rather softened when translated into drag ; third, the place to which we were directed to take the interesting young nun, and the persons assembled there, as I supposed, to condemn her. My fears were such, concerning the fate that awaited her, and my horror at the idea that she was in some way to be sacrificed, that I would have given anything to be allowed to stay where I was. But I feared the consequences of disobeying the Superior, and proceeded with the rest towards the room for the examination of conscience. The room to which we were to proceed from that was in the second story, and the place of many a scene of a shameful nature. St. Frances had appeared melancholy for some time. I well knew she had cause, for she had been repeatedly subject to trials which I need not name, our common lot. When we reached the room where we had been bidden to seek her, I entered the door, my companions standing behind me, as the place was so small as hardly to hold five persons at a time. The young nun was standing alone, near the middle of the room: she was probably about twenty, with light hair, blue eyes, and a very fair complexion. I spoke to her in a compassionate voice, but at the same time with such a decided manner, that she comprehended my full meaning.

" St. Frances, we are sent for you." Several others spoke kindly to her, but two addressed her very harshly. The poor creature turned round with a look of meekness, and without even speaking a word, resigned herself to our hands The tears came into my eyes. I had not a moment's doubt that she considered her fate as sealed, and was already beyond the fear of death. She was conducted, or rather hurried to the staircase, which was near by, and then seized by her limbs and clothes, and in fact almost dragged upstairs, in the sense the Superior had intended. I laid my own hands upon her; I took hold of her too more gently indeed than some of the rest; yet I engaged and assisted them in carrying her. I could not avoid it. My refusal would not have saved her, nor prevented her being carried up; it would only have exposed me to some severe punishment, as I believe some of my companions would have seized the first opportunity to complain of me.

All the way up the staircase, St. Frances spoke not a word, nor made the slightest resistance. When we entered with her the room to which she was ordered, my heart sank within me. The Bishop, the Lady Superior, and five priests, viz., Bonin, Richards, Savage, and two others, I now ascertained, were assembled for trial, on some charge of great importance.

When we had brought our prisoner before them, Father Richards began to question her, and she made ready but calm replies. I cannot pretend to give a connected account of what ensued; my feelings were wrought up to such a pitch, that I knew not what I did, or what to do; I was under a terrible apprehension that, if I betrayed the feelings which overcame me, I should fall under the displeasure of the cold-blooded persecutors of my poor innocent sister; and this fear on the one hand, with the distress I felt for her on the other, rendered me almost frantic. As soon as I entered the room, I had stepped into a corner, on the left of the entrance, where I might partially support myself by leaning against the wall, between the door and the window. This support was all that prevented me from falling to the floor, for the confusion of thoughts was so great, that only a few words I heard spoken on either side made any lasting impression upon me. I felt as if struck with some insupportable blow, and death would not have been more frightful to me. I am inclined to the belief, that Facher Richards wished to shield the poor prisoner from the severity of her fate by drawing from her expressions that might bear a favourable construction. He asked her, among other things, if she was now sorry for what she had been overheard to say (for she had been betrayed by one of the nuns) and if she would not prefer confinement in the cells to the punishment which was threatened. But the Bishop interrupted him, and it was easy to perceive that he considered her fate as sealed, and was determined that she should not escape. In reply to some of the questions put to her, she was silent; to others I heard her voice reply, that she did not repent the words she had uttered, though they had been reported by some of the nuns, who had heard them; that she had firmly resolved to resist every attempt to compel her to the commission of crimes which she detested.

"That is enough; finish her!" said the Bishop.

Two nuns instantly fell upon the woman, and in obedience to directions given by the Superior, prepared to execute her sentence. She still maintained all the calmness and submission of a lamb. Some of those who took part in the transaction, I believe, were as unwilling as myself; but of others, I can safely say, that they delighted in it. Their conduct certainly exhibited a most blood-thirsty spirit. But above all others present, and above all human fiends I ever saw, I think St. Hypolite was the most diabolical; she engaged in the horrid task with all alacrity, and assumed from choice the most revolting parts to be performed. She seized a gag, forced it into the mouth of the poor nun; and when it was fixed between her extended jaws, so as to keep them open at their greatest possible distance, took hold of the straps fastened at the end of the stick, crossed them behind the helpless head of the victim, and drew them tight through the loop prepared as fastening. The bed, which had always stood in one part of the room, still remained there, though the screen which had usually been placed before it, and was made of thick muslin, with only a crevice through which a person behind might look out, had been folded upon its hinges in the form of a W., and placed in a corner. On the bed the prisoner was laid with her face upward, and then bound with cords so that she could not move. They all did what they could, not only to smother, but to bruise her. Some stood up and jumped upon the poor girl with their feet; and others, in different ways, seemed to seek how they might best beat the breath out of her body, and mangle it, and without coming in direct contact with it, or seeing the effects of their violence. During the time my feelings were almost too strong to be endured. I felt stupefied, and scarcely was conscious of what I did. Still, fear for myself remained in a sufficient degree to induce me to some exertion; and I attempted to talk to those who stood next, partly that I might have an excuse for turning away from the dreadful scene.

NOSEGAYS AND BIRCHING.

Mr. D., a gentleman of fortune, excessively fond of the rod, advertised for a governess to instruct his three daughters, their French governess having returned to Paris.

Miss F., a young Irish lady, very pretty, and very much reduced, applied for the post.

Mr. D., finding her a great advocate for the rod, engaged her immediately. She was the daughter of Mrs. F., a schoolmistress in Dublin. Educated under such a mother, Miss F. was complete mistress of birch discipline, and as passionately fond of it as any woman in England.

A few days after she had been at Mr. D.'s seat, as she was going early in the morning to take a walk in the garden, Mr. D. perceived and followed her. She was in a half-morning dress, with a large French nightcap, her hair very large and low behind. Their conversation chiefly turned on the sweet perfume of the flowers; the gentleman proposed to make a nosegay for her sweet angelic bosom, and in a few minutes presented her with one as big as a broom. Miss F. was quite delighted with it, and instantly tied it very high on the left side of her bosom, for she was very well acquainted with their influence.

She thought it was now high time to introduce the favourite subject. She informed him that one of his nieces had been very bold, and that she intended to whip her. Mr. D. apologised for the trouble she would be at. "Don't talk of that, my dear Sir, I like to whip bold girls, especially when I can get a good birch-rod." Mr. D. conducted her to the shrubbery, where there were several birch-trees. She immediately made two excellent rods, and of large size, which sound very pleasing to the votaries of whipping, and gives a woman a severe air; besides, large rods do not hurt so much as small ones. As soon as she came to the house she went to the working-room, and calling the young culprit to her, a girl about thirteen, said, "Here is, Miss (shaking her big rod), something that shall make you good! Come, come, kiss the rod, and beg a good whipping." Then holding her upon her lap, she whipped her for full ten minutes. Mr. D. had never seen a woman whip with so much grace! Her dress, especially her monstrous bouquet, which she was smelling all the while, made her look most charming.

A SCEANCE.

"A likely story, indeed! Pack up your things, and leave this house at once. To-morrow I shall go to the village, pay your wages to Mrs. Lobkins, and let her know the reason why I turned you off."

Now this was what Charlotte most dreaded. Mrs. Lobkins, her mother, was a sour-visaged, strong-armed Methodist, who, having few weaknesses of her own to recall, had no mercy on her children's faults, and never spared the correction King Solomon enjoined, She enlarged even on the text, the "rod" in her Draconian code being merely child's play. Over the mantelpiece she kept *in terrorem* three supple bamboo canes, lashed together at one end. Having first let down their smocks, and tied their hands to the bedpost, she would belabour the backs of Lottie and her sisters until she was tired out with the exercise.

When the maiden thought of what was in store for her it curdled the marrow in her bones. "O, Miss Heleanor! you that was always so good and kind. I know I must go; but you said as I wasn't bright at my needle, let mother think it's for that; she'd kill me if she knew the truth."

"And do you imagine I am going to let wickedness like yours be concealed to save you from a beating? Begone, and pack up your things."

"Mercy, Miss Heleanor? Punish me yourself the way you would Master Willie—only worse; for I didn't ought to 'ave let let 'im hin."

Miss Davenport paused. Here was the creature at her mercy, and the rod at hand.

"Charlotte Lobkins," she said solemnly, "what you ask is no light thing: by one or the other you must be punished as your crime deserves. I know the kind of beating you get at home, and they are scarcely too bad for the present act. If I were to intercede for you with your mother, and promise to take you back a month hence, would you allow yourself to be whipped with a birch rod without disturbing the house with your cries?"

"And you won't tell mother what I done?"

"Not if you obey my orders now."

The punishment was then duly administered, and the exercise afforded much relief to the outraged virtue of Miss Davenport.

EXTRACT FROM *THE RODIAD.*

BY GEORGE COLMAN.

Oh ye who still hold FLAGELLATION dear,
Maintain it bravely each in his own sphere;
Parents, schoolmasters, guardians do your best
Never to let the ROD in torpor rest—
Extend the practice, propagate the zest;
Flog at all times, in every novel mode,
Instruct your teachers in the BUSHBY CODE,
Show how when gratified this appetite
Conduces to the comforts of the night;
And the wife's favour you will soon enlist,
Who finds the more he flogs, the more she's kissed,
Let every nurse have license free and large,
To scarify her juveniles in charge;
And make each nursery, in its form and rule,
A real PREPARATORY FLOGGING SCHOOL.
Let children take it as the natural thing,
Early to taste the birch's simple sting;
While canes and cats, and various whips impart
Their own experiences of all kinds of smart;
Shall I complain? When better hope is past,
FLOG and be flogged—is no bad fate at last.

FINIS.

www.ingramcontent.com/pod-product-compliance
Lightning Source LLC
Chambersburg PA
CBHW031447280326
41927CB00037B/386
* 9 7 8 1 4 1 0 1 0 3 8 3 3 *